Margaret Fulton
favourites

Margaret Fulton
favourites

The much-loved, essential
recipes from a lifetime of cooking

Margaret Fulton
Suzanne Gibbs

Photography by Tanya Zouev

hardie grant books
MELBOURNE · LONDON

✴✴✴ Cookery ✴✴

Contents

Introduction

'Fish please,' a small but assured voice piped up to the bemused waiter. My parents and older siblings could hardly believe their ears and burst into peals of laughter. I was three years old. Until then I had seldom uttered a word, let alone with such confidence.

Back then none of us could imagine how food would end up shaping my life. Growing up in country New South Wales we were lucky to have access to wonderful lamb, beef, poultry, raised as it should be, fresh garden vegetables and fruit from local orchards. And I was lucky to grow up with the sublime food that came out of my mother's kitchen. Her desire to cook delicious meals for her family was matched by her determination to obtain the best-quality produce.

My fascination with food and early indoctrination into mealtime preparation — necessary in a family of eight — set me firmly on a path towards a life of food and cooking. I have been able to spread the word that cooking is a most rewarding pleasure. Knowing a little about the background traditions, places and people behind a dish opens up a whole new world of interest and understanding.

Travel has had a huge influence on the way I view food and on the food that I cook. I have spent many working holidays overseas, and the best part has always been returning home with a wonderful fund of information and recipes from other cooks and nations. I first visited China in the 1970s, and remember learning from young chefs and also venerable masters. In the rural communes I was introduced to the most simple but beautiful foods — locally caught carp steamed with the finest angel hairs of ginger and aromatics — as refined as any dish in a top restaurant. I have equally fond memories of trips to India, where the food, people and customs simply captured my imagination. Today I often yearn for Indian food, but am also influenced by the wide and varied cuisines of Malaysia, Thailand, France, Italy, Spain and Scandinavia, having watched, and learnt from, the best local cooks in these places.

I enjoy making the French dishes I learnt when studying a course based on the great French master of the kitchen Auguste Escoffier. And I still cook with the French copper saucepans I bought in Paris more than 50 years ago.

For this book, I have sorted through a lifetime of recipes and chosen those I thought best and most representative of a half-century of cooking: the food I cook regularly, the dishes my family and friends like, and the recipes that readers have asked me for time and time again. All the love, experience and knowledge garnered from my family, and from people all over the world make up a big part of this book.

My kitchen has always been a happy place for me, my family and friends. Cooking together brings such joy — I loved the hours spent in the kitchen with my mother as a child, shelling peas, kneading dough and helping stir the pot, and I continued this tradition with my own daughter, Suzanne. It's been a pleasure to work alongside Suzanne on this and a number of cookbooks. I hope you enjoy the stories, food and recipes from my kitchen as much as we have in putting this book together.

Margaret Fulton

Soups, Starters
and Appetisers

I do love soup. I always have. Real homemade soup is so rarely served these days that when it is encountered it is truly welcomed by those who appreciate good food.

Soups are so easy to prepare and, because they can be created ahead of time, make mealtimes a great deal simpler if you lead a busy life. Any vegetable can be lightly sautéed in butter or oil and then cooked with stock before being puréed to make a great-tasting soup — the possibilities are endless.

Go to the effort of making a big batch of stock, then freeze it in recipe-size portions in plastic containers so that the stock is ready to use at any time. Or keep packets of concentrated stock on hand — the next best thing in terms of quality. A word of advice when using commercial stocks is to go easy on the seasoning, especially salt.

All soups benefit from a finishing touch — chopped herbs, a slice of lemon, a swirl of cream, a nut of butter or a sprinkling of crunchy croutons — a little something to say, 'this is special'.

Whole Chicken and Leek Soup

Like most Scots, I take the making of soup very seriously. Cock-a-leekie, or whole chicken and leek soup, is a close relative of the famous Jewish chicken soup — that wonderfully comforting cure-all otherwise known as 'Jewish penicillin'.

In the Scottish version, rice or barley is sometimes substituted for potatoes, and while the dish is almost always made with an older bird — what we call a 'boiler' — for best results spend a little extra and get an organic, free-range one.

1 size 15 (1.5 kg) chicken water or Chicken
  Stock (page 237)
1 onion, peeled
1 carrot, cut into chunks
2 stalks celery, sliced
3 leeks, trimmed, washed, then cut into
  thick slices
2 tablespoons rice, or 2 medium potatoes,
  peeled and diced
salt and freshly ground black pepper
1 cup broken egg noodles (optional)
2 tablespoons chopped flat-leaf parsley

SERVES 6

Wash the chicken inside and out. Place in a large saucepan with enough water or chicken stock to cover. Add the onion, bring to the boil, skim the surface and simmer, covered, for 30 minutes. Add the carrot and celery to the soup together with the leeks, and the rice or potatoes. Season with salt.

Simmer a further 15 minutes until tender, adding the noodles for the last 10 minutes, if using. Remove the chicken, draining well. Remove the wing joints and skin, and cut the flesh into bite-size pieces from the bones. Return the chicken flesh to the saucepan. Remove the onion and discard. Check the broth for seasoning, adding more salt if necessary.

Ladle into large soup bowls. Garnish with parsley and season with a good grinding of pepper. Serve with crusty bread if you like.

TIP - Keep the skin, bones and carcass of the chicken to make a second stock; it won't be as rich as the first, but is well worth making. Add these trimmings to any leftover stock with more water to cover and cook for an hour or so before straining.

Country Supper Soup

This is the way I have always made a family winter soup, and still do. I like to make a big pot of it. Some I put into screw-top jars for my granddaughter Louise to take down to her farm at weekends. It's a welcome gesture, as they arrive lateish on a Friday night after work and a long drive.

If I am too busy to cook the beans I use canned ones, sometimes chickpeas — whatever is in the pantry — drained and rinsed first. Essential to the soup, though, is a good homemade stock.

½ cup dried cannellini beans or
   1 x 400 g can cannellini beans, drained
bouquet garni (below)
30 g butter
1 clove garlic, crushed
2 medium onions, cut into large dice
2 medium carrots, peeled and cut into large dice
4 medium potatoes, peeled and cut into
   large dice
4 stalks celery, sliced
salt and freshly ground black pepper
2 tablespoons plain flour
9 cups Chicken Stock (page 237)
1 bay leaf
1 sprig each thyme and marjoram
½ cup chopped flat-leaf parsley
parmesan cheese, grated (optional)

SERVES 8

If using dried beans, soak them overnight in cold water to cover. Drain the beans, then put into a saucepan with a bouquet garni and enough water to cover. Bring slowly to the boil on medium heat, reduce the heat and simmer very gently for 45 minutes, until tender. Drain.

Melt the butter in a large saucepan over a low heat and cook the garlic and vegetables, covered, very gently for 15 minutes, stirring once or twice. This is called 'sweating' the vegetables; their flavour infuses the butter. Season with salt and pepper and stir in the flour. Cook for another 2 minutes, stirring gently. Add the stock, stirring, then the bay leaf and herbs. Stir until slightly thickened, then add the drained beans. Simmer, half-covered, for another 20 minutes.

Check for seasoning, adding more salt and pepper if necessary, and stir in the parsley. Ladle into warm soup bowls and offer, if you like, a bowl of grated parmesan cheese for people to sprinkle over their soup.

Bouquet garni
Place 5 peppercorns inside a short piece of celery, securing with a small piece of carrot, a few sprigs of fresh thyme and parsley, and a bay leaf. Tie up with string and use it to flavour stocks, stews and casseroles. Remove before serving food.

Tomato Saffron Soup

I first tasted saffron in Spain. It is used extensively in Spanish cooking, particularly for paella. As I was an official guest in the country, a guide took me to places of interest. In one picturesque village I found saffron threads — stigmas of the crocus flower — and because they seemed so inexpensive I bought them everywhere we stopped, enough to last for years. My guide gently informed me later that I had bought enough for a whole village's supply for one year. It wasn't said in criticism but I felt embarrassed and could hardly believe my greed. However, when I returned home I did share the saffron and didn't waste a bit of it.

This is a fresh look at an old favourite; tomato soup takes on a special flavour with this infusion of saffron and vermouth. The soup can be made well ahead and reheated at the last moment, with the fresh tomato, saffron and vermouth added at the end.

8 ripe vine-ripened tomatoes
a good pinch of saffron threads
¼ cup dry vermouth
30 g butter
1 medium onion, sliced
4 cups Chicken or Vegetable Stock
  (pages 237, 239)
1 small bay leaf
1 teaspoon sugar
salt and freshly ground black pepper
2 tablespoons cornflour
1 tablespoon cold water
2 tablespoons chopped flat-leaf parsley
a little olive oil

SERVES 4

Quarter 4 of the tomatoes and roughly chop them. Peel, seed and dice the remaining tomatoes (see Tip) and set aside. Combine the saffron and vermouth and set aside. Melt the butter in a saucepan over a gentle heat, add the onion, cover, and cook for 5 minutes, until softened. Add the roughly chopped tomatoes, stock, bay leaf, sugar, and salt and pepper to taste. Stir until boiling, then simmer for 20–30 minutes.

Pass the soup through a sieve, pour it back into the saucepan and reheat. Add the cornflour blended with the tablespoon of water to the soup and stir until slightly thickened.

To finish, stir in the saffron and vermouth with the diced tomatoes and heat gently. Ladle the soup into heated bowls. Garnish with parsley and a swirl of olive oil.

TIP - To peel and seed the tomatoes, place them in a bowl and cover with boiling water. Count to eight for ripe tomatoes, 10 or more if less ripe. Transfer to a bowl of iced water. Make a cross in the skin at the base and carefully peel off the skin. Halve the tomatoes and flick out the seeds.

Wonton

I had my first lesson in making wonton in the 1950s. Lean Sun Low was a restaurant in Dixon Street in Sydney's Chinatown. Like in many Chinese restaurants, when there was a lull, staff would sit at one of the tables preparing food. As I was a curious, regular customer, they shared the secret of making the delicate morsels that were an essential ingredient in the short soup that I loved.

Wonton, which in Chinese means 'swallowing clouds', are boiled and served in a broth — short soup — or served in a broth with noodles — long and short soup. They can also be fried and served with sweet and sour sauce, or shaped into money bags and steamed to become dim sim (steamed dumplings).

3 fresh or dried shiitake mushrooms
100 g green (raw) prawns, shelled, deveined
    and coarsely diced
125 g minced pork
2 tablespoons chopped spring onions
6 canned or freshly peeled water chestnuts,
    finely diced
1 teaspoon grated fresh ginger
1 tablespoon light soy sauce
½ teaspoon salt
250 g wonton wrappers
6–8 cups well-seasoned Chicken Stock
    (page 237)

MAKES ABOUT 30
SERVES 4–6

If using dried mushrooms, soak them in hot water for 30 minutes, then drain and discard stems. Slice the mushrooms finely. In a bowl combine the mushrooms, prawns, minced pork, spring onions, water chestnuts, ginger, soy sauce and salt. Mix well.

Place 1 teaspoon of mixture in the centre of each wrapper and moisten the edges with a little water. Fold in two diagonally, pressing the moistened edges together and using thumbs to press down on the pastry around the filling to secure and centre it. Next, fold one of the corners from the long edge across and secure by moistening to the opposite fold. Each wonton should now be a triangle with three distinct corners, rather like a nurse's cap.

As each wonton is finished, place it on a tray lined with plastic wrap. At this point the wonton can be covered and refrigerated until ready to cook.

To cook, lower the wonton a few at a time into gently simmering stock in a large saucepan. Cook for 5 minutes, stirring a few times at the beginning, until the wonton rise to the surface. Drain using a slotted spoon. >>

Short soup

Ladle wonton and broth into bowls and serve garnished with a few chopped spring onions.

Long and short soup

While the wonton are cooking, prepare 1 packet of egg noodles. Have a large bowl of cold water and a large saucepan of boiling water ready. Loosen the noodles gently with your fingers. Lower the noodles into the boiling water for 30 seconds, stirring constantly with chopsticks. Lift the noodles out with tongs and plunge into cold water for 30 seconds, then lift out and place into boiling water again for 30 seconds, stirring constantly. Drain and transfer to serving bowls. Add the wonton and ladle the hot broth over. Sprinkle with 2 tablespoons of chopped spring onions and drizzle each serving with a little sesame oil.

Fried wonton

To fry wonton, fill a wok with 5 cm of oil and heat until hot. Carefully lower the wonton into the oil in small batches. When they are cooked, the wonton will be golden and will rise to the surface. Lift out with a slotted spoon and drain on paper towels. Serve piping hot with sweet and sour sauce.

Dim sim (steamed dumplings)

Prepare one quantity of wonton, but instead of folding each wonton wrapper diagonally, gently squeeze the wrapper around the filling to resemble a money bag. Repeat with remaining ingredients. Rub the base of each tier of a wooden steamer with a little oil and place the dim sim in the steamer, leaving a space between them.

Place the steamer in a wok or saucepan filled with about 3 cm of simmering water. Cover and steam for 15 minutes. Serve piping hot with light soy, chilli or sweet and sour sauce for dipping.

NOTE - Bamboo and metal steamers, available at Asian food stores, have three layers, so you can cook a large number of dumplings at one time. This is great for entertaining.

Chicken Coriander Soup

Back in the 1960s I was one of the first people in Australia to grow my own coriander from seeds. It was a revelation to grow something I had first tasted in salads, garnishes and sauces in South America. Now that it is so readily available I use coriander almost every day in salads and stir-fries, and it works really well in this beautiful, spicy soup. Using spices, chicken breast and rice, this soup has an Asian touch when coconut milk is added, or a western flavour when cream takes its place. Whichever you choose, any soup can only be as good as its stock, so I naturally recommend a good homemade chicken stock.

30 g butter
1 teaspoon ground coriander
1 teaspoon ground cumin
1 chicken breast fillet, skin removed,
    cut into small pieces
2 tablespoons plain flour
5 cups Chicken Stock (page 237), heated
juice of ½ lemon
salt and freshly ground black pepper
⅓ cup coconut milk or pouring cream
¾ cup cooked rice, long- or short-grain
    (see Tip)
¼ cup lightly snipped fresh
    coriander leaves

SERVES 6

Heat the butter in a saucepan over a gentle heat and stir in the coriander, cumin and chicken pieces, cooking gently for 1 minute.

Remove from the heat, add the flour, stir and return to the heat. Cook for another minute then add the stock. Stir until blended and cook for another 5–6 minutes. Add the lemon juice, and salt and pepper to taste. Stir in the coconut milk or pouring cream and the cooked rice.

When the soup is heated through, add the coriander leaves and leave to stand for a minute or two before serving.

TIP - To prepare the rice, bring 1 cup of water to the boil, add a pinch of salt and 2 tablespoons of rice, then reduce heat and cook until the water evaporates — 10–12 minutes. Turn off the heat, cover and leave for a further 5 minutes. Fluff up the rice with a fork before adding it to the soup.

Tom Kha Gai

Rebecca Hsu Hui Min, the cooking queen of Hong Kong in the 1960s and 1970s, was a great influence in my early career. I knew something about Cantonese food from my regular visits to Sydney's Chinatown but she introduced me to hot and spicy northern Chinese food. I quickly took to the hot and sour taste of dishes like Sichuan Chicken Salad (page 172) and other South-East Asian food, such as Thailand's Tom Kha Gai (chicken soup). The sourness of the limes, heat of the red birdseye chillies, sharpness of the lemongrass and the kaffir lime leaves give this soup a lovely taste and fragrance.

3 cups Chicken Stock (page 237)
2 stalks lemongrass, tender parts cut into
   thin diagonal slices
2 kaffir lime leaves
3 slices galangal, cut into thin matchsticks
   (optional)
6 straw or button mushrooms, sliced
½ teaspoon salt
3 tablespoons lime juice
2 tablespoons fish sauce
2 chicken breast fillets, skin removed,
   cut into strips
2 cups coconut milk
1–2 red birdseye chillies, split and seeded
coriander leaves, to garnish

SERVES 4–6

Place the chicken stock in a large saucepan, add the lemongrass, lime leaves, galangal (if using), mushrooms and salt and bring slowly to the boil, then reduce heat. Add the lime juice, fish sauce and chicken strips and simmer uncovered for about 5 minutes, then add the coconut milk and chillies. Bring slowly back to the boil, stirring. Do not cook too quickly after adding the coconut milk — this should prevent the coconut milk from separating. Ladle into soup bowls and garnish with coriander.

TIP ~ Galangal looks like ginger (and they are indeed from the same family) but the two are not interchangeable. Many greengrocers and supermarkets sell galangal and kaffir lime leaves.

French Onion Soup

There was a time when no stay in Paris was complete without an early morning visit to Les Halles, the markets where the produce of France was scrutinised and bargained for before being carted off to the great restaurants of the city. It was at Les Halles that French onion soup, or soupe à l'oignon, was created. It was served in the many small bistros nearby to sustain the workmen who toiled at the markets through the wee small hours and the truck drivers who drove halfway across France with the produce. Les Halles is now a shopping centre and the huge professional market has been moved to Rungis in the eastern suburbs of Paris.

When I was living with my sister Jean on the Hawkesbury River in New South Wales we would often turn the soup into a more substantial meal in cold weather by cooking it in gratinée form, which to many is the real French onion soup.

45 g butter
1 tablespoon light olive oil
3 large onions, thinly sliced
1 teaspoon salt
2 teaspoons plain flour
7 cups Beef Stock (page 237)
½ cup dry white wine
freshly ground black pepper
rounds of baguette, cut into 2.5 cm slices
    for serving

SERVES 6

Melt the butter with the oil in a large heavy saucepan. Add the onions and cook them very gently until softened and golden, stirring occasionally. Do not allow them to brown. Sprinkle with salt and stir in the flour. When blended, cook over a medium heat for 3 minutes. Remove from the heat and stir in the stock. Add the wine and season with pepper. Cover the saucepan and simmer for 30–40 minutes, skimming the surface of the soup occasionally.

Preheat the oven to 160°C (320°F). While the soup is cooking, bake the bread slices on a baking sheet until crisp and lightly coloured. If desired, remove bread after 10 minutes, brush with a little olive oil and return to the oven for a further 5–10 minutes. You can also rub each slice lightly with a cut clove of garlic after baking. Serve with the soup.

French Onion Soup Gratinée

The French seem to enjoy eating after the theatre, or after a night out on the town. That's when this much-loved onion soup comes into its own. In top restaurants or bistros this soup is served in pottery bowls that can go under the salamander — that's the restaurant griller — or in the oven. The soup holds a thick slice of bread, toasted and topped with cheese, which floats to the top.

1 quantity French Onion Soup (opposite)
rounds of baguette, baked or toasted
250 g gruyère or emmental cheese,
    finely sliced or grated

SERVES 6

Bring the soup to the boil. Place prepared bread in an ovenproof soup tureen or in bowls. Pour boiling soup over the bread. Scatter the cheese over the top and place under a hot grill until the cheese melts and browns lightly. Serve immediately.

Mussel and Parsley Soup

All it took was a telephone call from Suzanne. 'Mum, the kids are going to the fish markets, would you like them to get some mussels for lunch?' My reply was prompt: 'Sure, and would you like me to show you how I make the mussel soup you all rave about?'

The kids (who are actually adults) were back with the mussels as I arrived with a loaf of sourdough bread, and then it was all action. Everyone had a job — setting the table, scrubbing the mussels, chopping onions and parsley, or keeping the cats away. I love the atmosphere of everyone across the generations working together, bonded by a common love — eating good food.

Mussels are quite cheap and make a great meal. But you have to be choosy. Try to get fairly small ones — preferably Australian cultivated mussels — that feel heavy for their size. This is a great soup for a fun and relaxed gathering.

2 kg mussels
3 tablespoons olive oil
2 onions, chopped
¾ cup verjuice or 1 cup dry white wine
　(see Tips overleaf)
1½ cups sourdough breadcrumbs
　(see Tips overleaf)
½ cup chopped flat-leaf parsley
freshly ground black pepper

SERVES 6

Scrub the mussels well in several changes of water. Tug off the beards and rinse the mussels thoroughly. Place the mussels in a large saucepan with ½ cup of water and steam, covered, shaking the pan occasionally, for 4–6 minutes, or until the shells have opened. Drain the mussels in a colander set over a bowl, reserving the liquid. Strain the reserved liquid through a fine sieve into a large measuring jug. Add enough water to the liquid to measure 6 cups altogether. Remove the mussels from the shells and, if you like, leave a few with shells to garnish. Discard shells and set mussels aside.

In a large heavy-based saucepan, heat the oil and cook the onions for 5 minutes, stirring, until softened. Add the reserved mussel liquid and verjuice or wine and bring slowly to the boil, then add breadcrumbs and simmer gently for about 10 minutes. Add the parsley and pepper, and continue to simmer gently for another minute without letting the soup boil. Stir in the mussels to reheat them and then serve.　>>

Mussel and parsley soup with cream

Make one quantity of mussel and parsley soup. When adding water to reserved liquid, make 5 cups altogether and add 1 cup of cream.

Mussel and parsley soup with wine (mussels marinière)

Make one quantity of mussel and parsley soup using only a good-quality white wine (no verjuice) and only 3–4 tablespoons of freshly made breadcrumbs. The opened mussels are left in their shells and a squeeze of lemon juice adds a fresh tang. In France, diners take off the top mussel shell and use it to scoop up the mussel still in the shell. Serve some crusty bread to mop up the juices.

Mussel and parsley soup with tomatoes

Make one quantity of mussel and parsley soup with wine but do not add water to the wine. Add 2 peeled, seeded and diced tomatoes, a nut of butter and one chopped clove of garlic.

TIPS ~ Verjuice is the unfermented juice of unripe grapes and can be used in the same way as lemon juice, vinegar or wine to add a piquancy to dishes.

Make fresh breadcrumbs by whizzing small pieces of stale sourdough bread in a food processor. If sourdough is not available, use any bread.

Leek and Potato Soup

In the hands of the practical French, leek and potato soup takes on another guise. By puréeing it, the soup becomes potage parmentier; by chilling it, and with the addition of cream, it can be turned into a beautiful summer soup called vichyssoise.

I have always been intrigued by the story of Louis Diat, one of the great French chefs, who travelled to London and New York to cook his wonderful food for the rich and famous. He loved the leek and potato soup made from his grandmother's recipe and served it at his restaurant (the famous Ritz-Carlton). During a heatwave in New York he knew the soup would not be enjoyed, so he chilled it and finished it with a swirl of cream. Voilà! Vichyssoise was born.

60 g butter
2 onions, finely sliced
3 leeks, trimmed, washed, then cut into
    thick slices
2 medium potatoes, peeled and diced
6 cups Chicken Stock (page 237)
¾ cup white wine
salt and freshly ground black pepper
a little chopped flat-leaf parsley

SERVES 4–6

Melt the butter in a medium-sized saucepan, then add the onions, leeks and potatoes. Cook the vegetables very gently with the lid on until they are soft and pale golden. Add the stock and wine and simmer for 8–10 minutes. Season with salt and pepper and serve garnished with parsley.

Potage parmentier

Prepare one quantity of leek and potato soup. Purée in an electric blender or food processor fitted with a double-sided steel blade, a few cupfuls at a time, or pass through a sieve. Reheat and lighten the soup with 4 tablespoons of cream or 30 g of butter. Serve hot, sprinkled with parsley or croutons.

Vichyssoise

Make potage parmentier, omitting the butter or cream added at the end of the cooking time. Allow the soup to cool after it is puréed, then stir in 1 cup of cream. Chill and check for seasoning, adding more salt and pepper if necessary. To serve, top with a spoonful of whipped or thick cream or swirl in a little light cream, and sprinkle with snipped chives or parsley. Vichyssoise can also be served hot.

Chicken Liver Pâté

Liver has outstanding nutritional properties and I like to include it in my family meals at least once a week. A favourite way is to make this easy and simple pâté. It is delicious smeared on crisp biscuits, Lavash (page 33), crusty bread or slices of Melba toast as a pre-dinner appetiser.

500 g chicken livers
155 g butter
2 tablespoons finely sliced shallots
1 clove garlic, finely sliced
1 bay leaf
1 sprig thyme
salt and freshly ground black pepper
2 tablespoons brandy
2 tablespoons chicken fat or butter

SERVES 6–8

Examine the chicken livers and remove any dark spots and sinews. Heat 1 tablespoon of the butter in a frying pan. Add the shallots and garlic and fry gently until softened. Add the chicken livers to the pan with the bay leaf and thyme. Season with salt and pepper and fry for 3–5 minutes, until the livers are stiffened and lightly browned but still pink inside.

Remove the bay leaf and thyme and blend the livers in a food processor or blender in 2 batches. Cream the remaining butter and gradually beat into the liver paste. Add the brandy to the pan in which the livers were cooked and reduce over a high heat to 1 tablespoon. Fold into the liver mixture, check for seasoning and spoon into a terrine dish or individual ramekins.

Cut the chicken fat into small pieces and melt in a pan over low heat. Alternatively, melt the butter. Strain the fat or butter into a jug and pour over the pâté to prevent it from oxidising. Refrigerate for several hours before eating. The pâté will keep for 1 week. Serve with Melba toast or toast fingers.

Melba toast

Toast fairly thin slices of bread until golden. Remove the crusts, if you wish, and while the toast is still hot, split each slice through the centre. This is easy when the toast is warm. If using square sandwich bread, cut each slice into 2 triangles.

Preheat the oven to 190°C (375°F). Arrange the slices, cut-side up, on trays and bake for about 5 minutes until they curl slightly and are golden. Cool then store in an airtight container.

Chicken Liver Parfait

I wouldn't want to live anywhere else in the world but if I could wave a magic wand I'd like to regularly transport myself to France, where I would set about finding the nearest charcutière (butcher). 'Charcuterie' is French for 'cooked meat', and describes the processing of sausages, cured meats, hams, terrines and pâté.

I miss my late friend restaurateur Anders Ousback — his keen intellect, sharp wit and wonderful sense of humour. He would constantly bring me little treasures. Chicken liver parfait was one of his regular gifts. We would share it over a glass or two of whisky or a glass of wine. So, to keep up the tradition, I make my own parfait for special occasions.

500 g chicken livers
1 medium onion, finely diced
500 g butter, melted
1 teaspoon thyme leaves
1 bay leaf
1 teaspoon rosemary leaves
3 cloves garlic, peeled
⅓ cup red wine
⅓ cup brandy
⅓ cup port
4 eggs
1 teaspoon salt
1 teaspoon freshly ground
   black pepper

SERVES 6–8

Trim the chicken livers well of all sinew using kitchen scissors and then cut each in half. In a medium-sized pan, gently cook the onion with 2 tablespoons of the melted butter until softened. Add the herbs, garlic, red wine, brandy and port and bring to the boil. Simmer over a moderate heat until reduced to a thick syrupy glaze. Cool and remove the bay leaf.

Preheat the oven to 180°C (350°F). Pour the glaze into a food processor fitted with a metal blade and add the chicken livers, eggs and remaining butter, reserving some of the butter to spoon over the top later. Season well with salt and freshly ground pepper.

Process until very smooth, then spoon the mixture into individual ovenproof ramekins. Place the dishes in a baking pan and fill the pan with boiling water until it reaches halfway up the height of the ramekins. Cover with a sheet of baking paper and bake for 45–50 minutes.

Remove from the oven, leave to cool, then pour a little of the reserved melted butter onto each ramekin to seal the parfait from the air. Refrigerate for several hours at least before eating. Serve with crackers, thin toast, crusty bread or lavash.

Lavash

Suzanne's husband, Robert, loves to make lavash (sometimes called lavoche). He bakes the lavash in large sheets, which he breaks up to serve, usually with an accompanying bowl of Chicken Liver Pâté (page 30) or Tapenade (page 34). You can buy lavash in delis or gourmet food stores but they are a breeze to make yourself and the result is every bit as good, if not better.

Lavash are great for entertaining when arranged in a napkin-lined basket alongside a pâté or a bowl of dip, or as a base for a lovely cheese platter.

2 cups plain flour
1½ teaspoons sea salt
1 teaspoon sugar
2 tablespoons poppy seeds
2 tablespoons sesame seeds
1 egg, lightly beaten
1 cup milk
60 g unsalted butter, melted

MAKES ABOUT 100 5 X 3 CM CRACKERS

Sift the flour, salt and sugar into a large mixing bowl and stir in the poppy and sesame seeds. Make a well in the centre and add the egg, followed by the milk and melted butter. Slowly incorporate the flour into the liquids to form a dough.

Knead the dough lightly on a floured board, then wrap in plastic wrap and chill for an hour or so.

Preheat the oven to 180°C (350°F). Cut the dough into quarters and roll very thinly, one piece at a time, to 10 x 40 cm rectangles — it doesn't matter if you get a few holes. Cut across into serving-size rectangles or leave in large pieces to break up later, when they are cooked. Place on baking trays and bake for 8 minutes, until dry and pale golden. Transfer to wire racks to cool and store in an airtight container.

Making a cheese platter

A selection of two cheeses is usually sufficient, one hard and the other soft or blue. They should be left out of the refrigerator long enough to come to room temperature before eating. Serve with a few muscatels or other dried or glacé fruits, and fresh fruit such as grapes, pears or apples.

Tapenade

People have been cultivating olives for thousands of years. We eat them now for the same reasons we always have — for their flavour and nutritional value. We nibble olives with a drink; we add them to salads, stews and pizzas; we stuff them; we eat them green, purple, black — at all the different stages of ripeness. But one of the best things we do is make a paste with them, and one of the best pastes is the French tapenade.

Whether for a picnic, quick snack or a light lunch there is nothing nicer than a bowl of this delicious paste of olives, anchovies, capers and tuna. Serve with halved hard-boiled eggs, some crusty bread and a few crisp vegetables. Tapenade is all the better for being made a few days ahead and stored in an airtight container in the refrigerator.

200 g black olives, pitted
6 anchovy fillets, drained and rinsed
3 tablespoons capers, drained
1 x 100 g canned tuna in oil, drained
juice of 1 lemon
⅓ cup olive or sunflower oil
a few extra black olives, for serving

SERVES 6–8

Crush the olives in a mortar or chop in a food processor. Add the anchovy fillets, capers, tuna and half the lemon juice. Pound or process until the mixture has formed a fairly smooth paste.

While still pounding, or with the processor still running, add the oil in a slow, steady stream. Taste and add more lemon juice if liked. Transfer to a small serving bowl, decorate with a few black olives and serve.

Gougères

Gougères — delectable little puffs of feather-light choux pastry flavoured with gruyère cheese — hail from Burgundy in France and are one of my favourite things to serve with a glass of red wine.

You can make them ahead of time — shape them on a tray lined with baking paper and then freeze. When they are frozen they can be transferred into freezer bags ready for baking any time. Gougères become cheese beignets when deep-fried until puffed and golden.

To ensure they puff up properly, the dough should be cooled before beating in the eggs. At first the egg makes the dough separate into slippery clumps that don't want to mix, but keep going and the dough will eventually become smooth and shiny.

1 cup plain flour
1 cup water or milk, or a mixture of both
100 g unsalted butter
1 teaspoon sugar
½ teaspoon salt
4 eggs
100 g gruyère or other Swiss-style
   cheese, grated
a little beaten egg

MAKES 30–40

Preheat the oven to 200°C (400°F) and grease 2 baking trays. Sift flour onto a piece of greaseproof paper. Put the water and/or milk, butter, sugar and salt into a medium-sized saucepan. Bring to a rapid boil and, using the greaseproof paper as a funnel, pour the flour all at once into the boiling mixture. Over a gentle heat, incorporate the flour quickly and thoroughly with a wooden spoon and beat until the mixture balls around the spoon and leaves the sides of the pan (a bit of muscle is needed here). This process dries the paste and cooks the flour.

Remove from the heat, transfer the mixture to a bowl and cool. Beat in the eggs, one at a time, using an electric mixer with a paddle beater if you have one. If using a wooden spoon, beat each egg lightly first before adding. If the paste is very stiff, beat an extra egg and add gradually until a pliable consistency is obtained. Beat until well combined, shiny and smooth.

Add the cheese and mix lightly. Use 2 spoons to drop small balls of the mixture onto baking trays. Brush with a little beaten egg and bake for 20 minutes, until puffed and golden. Serve piping hot.

Olive Bread

I picked up this recipe on a visit to Venice many years ago, when the sight of black olives in bread was a really new idea to me. Now we often make it when we go to my granddaughter's farm; the smell of baking bread welcomes everyone and puts us in that country holiday mood.

The best way to serve it is cut into chunks for dunking into a good extra-virgin olive oil, or topped with a soft goat's cheese or curled slice of prosciutto. Olive bread also makes a lovely base for savoury sandwiches and is good just sliced with icy-cold butter or a dip like Baba Ghanouj (page 39)

4 cups plain flour
1 teaspoon sea salt
2 teaspoons sugar
1 sachet dry yeast
freshly ground black pepper
4 tablespoons olive oil
1½–2 cups warm water
¾ cup black olives, pitted and
  roughly chopped

SERVES 6–8

Sift the flour into a large bowl with the salt and sugar. Stir in the yeast. Make a well in the centre and add the pepper, olive oil and warm water.

Gradually incorporate the wet ingredients into the flour mixture. Mix to a soft manageable dough, adding more water if necessary. Turn onto a floured surface and knead for 5–10 minutes until the dough is smooth and elastic. Incorporate the olives until mixed through evenly. Place in a greased bowl and sprinkle with a few drops of water. Cover the bowl with plastic wrap, then a tea towel. Leave in a warm place for 1 hour.

Preheat the oven to 200°C (400°F). Grease and flour a baking tray. Lightly knead the dough again, and shape into 2 loaves, each 25 cm long. Place on the tray, sprinkle with a little flour and cover with a cloth. Leave for 15 minutes, until doubled in size, and make slashes on the tops of the loaves with a sharp knife.

Bake the loaves for 20 minutes then reduce the oven temperature to 180°C (350°F) and bake for another 25–30 minutes, until the bread sounds hollow when tapped and is well risen and golden.

Smoky Eggplant Caviar

Smoky eggplant caviar, also known as poor man's caviar, was created by the wives of the Beluga caviar fishermen in Russia who could never afford to eat the caviar they harvested for wealthy noblemen. It is a much more affordable topping for pieces of bread or toast than the real thing.

It gets its wonderful smoky flavour from the eggplants being charred under a hot grill or on a barbecue. Serve piled in bowls alongside Olive Bread (page 36), Lavash (page 33), sliced baguette or lightly toasted rounds of pita bread.

1 eggplant (about 500 g)
2 teaspoons lemon juice
1–2 cloves garlic, crushed (optional)
½ teaspoon salt
3–4 tablespoons natural yoghurt (optional)
salt and freshly ground black pepper
1 tablespoon olive oil

MAKES ABOUT 2 CUPS

Place the unpeeled, untrimmed eggplant under a very hot preheated griller. Turn the eggplant every 5 minutes until the skin is charred all over and the flesh is soft throughout. Alternatively, the eggplant may be 'smoked' over a very low gas flame, and turned frequently until the skin is charred. If you are cooking the eggplant on a barbecue, cook it until blackened, collapsed and cooked through.

Let the eggplant cool. Halve it and carefully scoop out the flesh into a mixing bowl, then mash with a fork. Add the remaining ingredients, whisking in the oil gradually with a fork until the mixture thickens, yet remains chunky. Adjust seasoning to taste.

NOTE - Some recipes suggest salting the eggplant before cooking, which I think is only necessary if you suspect it isn't as young at it should be (see Eggplant Parmigiana, page 53). If salting, halve eggplant lengthwise, score the cut side deeply and sprinkle liberally with salt.

Leave to drain, cut-side down, for at least 30 minutes. Rinse and pat dry with a paper towel.

To cook, lightly oil a baking dish, place the eggplant cut-side down in the dish and cook under a medium grill, turning from time to time, until tender and skin is charred. Leave to cool before scooping out the flesh while holding the stem.

Baba Ghanouj

If you like Lebanese food you will appreciate this recipe. I serve baba ghanouj on a flat plate, like an open soup plate, spread and then swirled with a spoon. I then sometimes add a splash of good-quality olive oil and some chopped parsley.

The tahini, lemon and garlic should not dominate but should meld into a rich, creamy, smoky whole. Tahini, a paste made from sesame seeds, lemon and garlic, is added gradually. Taste and stop adding when you have the flavour you like.

1 eggplant (about 500 g)
2 tablespoons lemon juice, or to taste
3–4 tablespoons tahini (sesame seed paste)
2 cloves garlic, crushed in a little sea salt
1 tablespoon olive oil
2 tablespoons chopped flat-leaf parsley

MAKES ABOUT 2 CUPS

Cook the eggplant as described in the previous recipe. Scoop out the flesh and mash the pulp with a fork. Gradually beat in the lemon juice alternately with the tahini. Add garlic, mix well and then transfer to a shallow serving bowl. Sprinkle with the oil and chopped parsley. Serve with pieces of Lebanese or pita bread.

TIP ~ Avoid the temptation to over-mash the baba ghanouj — pieces of eggplant should still be evident.

Salmon Gravlax

Gravlax is raw salmon, usually cured in a mixture of salt, sugar and alcohol. I use vodka, but other approaches call for more powerful spirits such as cognac or bourbon. This treatment, Scandinavian in origin, resembles the curing or smoking methods of preparing fish in Britain or Eastern Europe — though there is no smoke used here. It can be made using a whole fish, but at home you're probably better off with just two substantial fillets. It is usually sliced very thinly on the bias (a sharp slicing knife is essential) to reveal as much of the surface of the flesh as possible. While this is a very simple recipe, the curing takes three days, so plan ahead.

1 whole salmon, weighing at least 2 kg
½ cup sugar
½ cup salt
1 tablespoon crushed black peppercorns
1 medium bunch dill
3 tablespoons vodka
grated rind of 1 lemon

SERVES 10

Remove the fillet from each side of the salmon, or ask your fishmonger to do this for you, leaving the skin intact. Discard head and bones. Pat the salmon with damp paper towels. Remove any protruding pin bones (the bones that stick out of the middle of the fillet) with tweezers. Combine the sugar, salt and pepper and rub on both sides of the fillets.

You will need a ceramic dish wide enough for the fillets to lie flat in. Place about a third of the dill into the dish. Sprinkle the dill with 1 tablespoon vodka. Place one fillet, skin-side down, into the dish. Cover the fillet with a third of the dill, a tablespoon of vodka and half the lemon rind. Top with the second fillet, skin-side up. Match up the pieces so the thicker end of the top piece sits over the thinner end of the bottom one, making the neatest possible package.

Place the remaining dill on top of the fish along with the remaining tablespoon of vodka. Cover the fish completely in plastic wrap, very tightly. Weigh it down (without crushing it) with a heavy dish. Place the ceramic dish in the fridge and leave it for 3 days, turning the fish once daily. >>

To serve the gravlax, scrape away the seasonings and pat fish dry with a paper towel. Slice the flesh on the bias as thinly as possible without tearing it. Using the skin as your guide, slide the knife as close to it as possible (there should be no skin adhering to the slice).

Use long sawing strokes to make the slices. It's best if you can almost see through the fish. You will notice some dark meat against the rosy flesh; neatly cut it away because it is often too strong and fishy in flavour.

The salmon can be kept for 2–5 days in the fridge. Serve in thin slices as you would smoked salmon. Accompany with rye, black or other good bread and with sour cream and grated horseradish or dill sauce.

Dill Sauce

2 tablespoons Dijon mustard
2 tablespoons caster sugar
a pinch of salt
1 teaspoon white wine vinegar
⅓ cup light olive oil
2 tablespoons chopped dill
1 teaspoon lemon juice

MAKES ABOUT ½ CUP

Combine mustard, sugar and salt in a small bowl. Add vinegar and slowly whisk in the oil until slightly thickened. Add dill and lemon juice.

Salmon Mousse

In the 1970s, salmon mousse often featured on buffet tables or was served as a first course. Friends claim it is just as popular at their parties today as it was then. It gives you a chance to present and show off a beautifully decorated platter.

A good recipe stands the test of time and is often created by a good cook. This recipe was given to me by a London cookery writer who made it with fresh salmon, which was plentiful in England but not in Australia at the time. So I first made it with good canned red salmon, but today use fresh salmon now that it is readily available.

1 tablespoon gelatine
¼ cup water
2 teaspoons sugar
1 teaspoon salt
1 teaspoon dry mustard
¼ cup white vinegar
2 cups flaked red salmon, canned
  or poached (see Note)
1 cup finely diced celery
2 teaspoons capers
½ cup whipped cream
salad greens, to garnish

SOUR CREAM DRESSING
½ cup sour cream
1 tablespoon grated onion
½ teaspoon salt
freshly ground black pepper
1 teaspoon horseradish relish (optional)
2 teaspoons vinegar
a pinch of paprika

**SERVES 6–8 AS A FIRST COURSE
OR MORE AS PART OF A BUFFET**

Sprinkle the gelatine over the water in a small saucepan. Soak for 2 minutes. Add the sugar, salt, mustard and vinegar. Stir constantly over low heat until the gelatine is dissolved. Remove from the heat and chill to the consistency of unbeaten egg whites. Fold in the salmon, celery and capers, mix well and then fold in the whipped cream. Turn into a wetted 750 ml mould, or individual moulds, and chill until firm.

Unmould onto a serving plate and garnish with salad greens. Serve with sour cream dressing.

For the sour cream dressing, combine all ingredients except paprika in a bowl, then chill well. Sprinkle with paprika before serving.

NOTE – Gently poach 750 g fresh salmon in 1½ cups of water with ½ teaspoon of wine vinegar and 1 teaspoon of salt. I find a frying pan is ideal for this. Cover and poach for 3 minutes, then turn off the heat and leave until cool enough to handle. Remove the fish and flake into pieces, removing any bones or skin.

Piroshki

I learnt about this recipe for soft buns filled with onion and smoked bacon in the 1970s from a Russian reader of *Woman's Day*, when we were running a national bake-off. In those days the recipe seemed so exotic and different — sausage rolls being our closest equivalent. I'd never tasted anything so good and have been making them ever since. We, the judges, were so impressed that we awarded the piroshki a major prize. I have since found out that there are many variations to these Russian meat pies — they may contain mince or cabbage, and are often fried instead of baked — but this is still the recipe I like the best.

PASTRY

1¼ cups milk
125 g butter
2 tablespoons sugar
3 cups plain flour
2 teaspoons salt
1 sachet dry yeast
1 egg yolk
beaten egg, to glaze

FILLING

3 large onions, finely diced
60 g butter
250 g speck or smoked streaky
  bacon, finely diced
freshly ground black pepper

**MAKES 45–50 APPETISER-SIZE
OR 30 LARGE PIROSHKI**

Heat the milk, butter and sugar in a saucepan over a low heat, stirring occasionally, until lukewarm and the butter has melted. Sift the flour with the salt into a large mixing bowl. Stir in the yeast. Make a well in the centre and pour in the milk mixture and egg yolk. Stir with a wooden spoon, gradually incorporating the flour. Beat the dough for 3 minutes, until smooth and elastic. You can use your hands or the dough hook of an electric mixer. Sprinkle a little flour on top, cover with plastic wrap then a folded tea towel, and leave
in a warm place until doubled, about 1 hour.

Meanwhile, make the filling. Fry onions in butter over a low heat, stirring, until golden, then cool. Add the speck with a good grinding of pepper.

Preheat the oven to 230°C (445°F). Turn the dough out onto a floured surface, knead lightly, and pinch off a tablespoon-sized piece. Flatten it slightly into a thick disc and place a teaspoon of filling on top. Fold the edges over to enclose the filling and mould into a ball. Place on a lightly greased baking tray. Repeat with the remaining dough and filling, cover baking tray loosely with plastic wrap and leave in a warm place for 15 minutes. Brush with beaten egg and bake for 10–15 minutes, until golden and cooked.

Tiropetes

There was a time when we would have to travel miles to sample these delicious pastries. The skill and mystery of the fine, paper-like sheets we came to know as filo were beyond our conception. It was a great day when someone started making filo and taking it to a Greek pastry shop in our city. Soon the orders rolled in and filo could be found in the suburbs and then a big company took over making it and you could buy filo, fresh or frozen, as far away as Darwin. Then we could make own our tiropetes, as well as other pastry treats. Tiropetes are great for party nibbles; people love a crisp savoury nibble with a drink!

1 bunch English spinach
4 onions, finely diced
60 g butter
5 eggs, beaten
4 or 5 finely sliced spring onions, including
   a little of the green
250 g feta cheese, chopped
1 teaspoon ground nutmeg
1 cup finely chopped flat-leaf parsley
salt and freshly ground black pepper
250 g filo pastry
150 g unsalted butter, melted

MAKES ABOUT 48

Wash the spinach thoroughly and steam for about 5 minutes until tender. Drain well, cool and squeeze to remove any excess moisture. Chop fairly finely. Fry the onions gently in the butter until golden brown. In a bowl, combine the eggs, spring onions, cheese, nutmeg and parsley. Add the onions and spinach, and season with salt and pepper to taste. Leave the mixture to cool.

Lay the filo flat on a dry tea towel and cover with a second dry towel, then a damp tea towel so the pastry will not dry out. Preheat the oven to 190°C (375°F).

Lay one sheet of filo flat with the short end towards you and brush gently with the melted butter. Place another sheet on top of the first and brush again. Cut the double sheet lengthwise into 4 strips, each about 4 cm wide, depending on the size of the sheets. Place a tablespoon of the filling on a pastry strip at the end closest to you and fold the corner over it to make a triangle. Continue to fold the pastry strip up and over, in triangles, until you come to the top end of the pastry strip. Brush the top with more melted butter. Place on an ungreased baking tray and repeat with remaining pastry and filling. Bake in the preheated oven for 45 minutes, or until puffed and golden brown.

NOTE – Tiropetes can be assembled in advance, frozen, and baked when required.

Samosas

At sunset, many Indian families and friends gather together. It was at one such occasion in Assam that I was introduced to samosas. Under the shade of a great spreading tree, we nibbled at these crispy pastries containing subtly spiced fillings of meat and vegetables and sipped freshly made tea or iced gin and tonics. As I gazed at the sunset beyond the neat rows of the tea plantation bordered by jungle, I commented that it was the nearest I'd been to a jungle. My hosts replied, 'Oh, we'll get Raja to take you in tomorrow, you might see that tiger that's been hanging around, or at least a one-horned rhinoceros.' Imagine my surprise when I was taken to meet Raja — an enormous gentle elephant — for my first elephant ride into the jungle. When I want to relive the experience I make these samosas.

PASTRY

1 cup plain flour
½ teaspoon salt
1 tablespoon ghee or butter
3–4 tablespoons lukewarm water

FILLING

1 tablespoon ghee
2 cm piece green ginger, grated
2 onions, chopped
2 tablespoons chopped mint
2 teaspoons curry powder
1 teaspoon salt
250 g minced lamb
1 tomato, peeled and chopped
juice of ½ lemon
½ teaspoon garam masala
a little milk
oil for deep-frying

MAKES 24

To make the pastry, sift the flour and salt into a bowl. Rub in ghee or butter with fingertips. Add the water and knead the pastry in the bowl to form a stiff dough. Cover the bowl with a cloth and allow to stand while preparing the filling.

To make the filling, heat the ghee and gently fry the ginger, half the onions and all of the mint until the onions are soft and golden. Stir in the curry powder and salt and fry for 2–3 minutes. Add the lamb and cook for 5 minutes, stirring. Add tomato. Bring to the boil, reduce heat and cook, uncovered, for 30 minutes. Stir occasionally, until any moisture has evaporated. Add the lemon juice and garam masala. Cool and add remaining onions.

Divide the pastry into 12 even-sized pieces. Shape each into a ball and roll out on a lightly floured board to the size of a small saucer, keeping the shape round. Cut each circle in half and moisten the edges with milk. Place a small spoonful of filling on one side of the half-round and fold the other side over. Press the edges together well. If you like, roll and crimp the edges for a decorative effect.

Heat the oil in a heavy pan or wok and fry the samosas, a few at a time, until golden and puffed. Drain on paper towels and serve hot. Chilli sauce or chutney may be offered for dipping.

Vegetable Samosas

500 g potatoes, peeled
1 tablespoon ghee or oil
1 teaspoon brown or black mustard
    seeds (optional)
½ teaspoon ground turmeric
½ teaspoon chilli powder
1 teaspoon salt
1 green chilli, halved, seeded and sliced
2 tablespoons chopped mint or coriander leaves
lime or lemon juice
½ teaspoon garam masala
¾ cup cooked green peas or cauliflower
    florets (optional)
1 quantity samosa pastry (page 47)

MAKES 24

Boil the potatoes in salted water until almost tender and cut into small dice. Heat the ghee or oil and fry the mustard seeds, if using, until they pop in the pan — cover to prevent them jumping out. Add the turmeric and chilli powder and fry for a few seconds. Add the salt, chilli and potatoes. Remove from the heat, add the herbs, lime or lemon juice to taste, and garam masala. If using, add the peas or cauliflower florets to the potatoes. Use the mixture to fill the pastry as for the meat filling (page 47).

NOTE ~ Instead of making your own pastry, packet spring roll pastry can be used. This light pastry comes in various sizes. If frozen, thaw, peel off as many sheets as you need, reseal the packet and return to the freezer. Cut out circles using a large biscuit cutter, or use a saucer as a guide. Keep pastry covered with a damp tea towel to prevent it from drying out.

Light Meals

Eggplant Parmigiana

When I was a young mother in the 1950s I lived in a little cottage on the Hawkesbury River with my sister Jean and her author husband. Jean was a great gardener and grew Mediterranean vegetables such as eggplant and capsicum. She was one of the first people to grow basil in Australia. Naturally we were always looking for new and different ways to cook these novel vegetables — in those days only sold by a few Italian or Greek greengrocers. One of my favourite ways of cooking eggplant is to layer the cooked slices with tomato sauce and cheese. My granddaughter Louise often simplifies this dish by making individual portions, topping the fried eggplant slices with sliced tomato and mozzarella cheese, sprinkling it with parmesan and popping it under a hot griller until the cheese melts.

2 medium eggplants
salt
3 tablespoons flour
freshly ground black pepper
olive oil for frying
2 cloves garlic, crushed
500 g ripe tomatoes, peeled and diced
200 g mozzarella cheese, sliced
¼–½ cup grated parmesan cheese
basil or oregano leaves, to garnish

SERVES 4–6

Cut the eggplants into thick slices (this can be done lengthwise if you like). Arrange in a colander, sprinkling layers liberally with salt. Leave to drain for about 30 minutes, then rinse and pat dry. Dredge each slice in the flour seasoned with salt and pepper.

Heat a thin film of oil in a large frying pan over a medium heat. Fry the eggplant slices in batches, adding more oil when necessary, for several minutes on each side until golden and just tender.

Meanwhile, heat 2 tablespoons of oil in a saucepan and add the garlic and tomatoes. Cook over a brisk heat until the tomatoes are soft and thick, resembling a chunky sauce. Season with salt and pepper.

Preheat the oven to 190°C (375°F). Lightly oil a large ovenproof dish and spoon over one-third of the tomato sauce. Top with a layer of half the eggplant slices, one-third of the mozzarella and a sprinkling of parmesan cheese. Spoon over another third of the tomato sauce.

Top with remaining eggplant, half the remaining mozzarella and parmesan. Finish with the last of the tomato, mozzarella and parmesan. Bake for about 10 minutes, until cheese is melted and bubbling. Garnish with fresh basil or oregano leaves before serving.

Asparagus and Prosciutto Frittata

Forty years ago I had a Spanish woman working for me who often included me in her family festivities. There would always be a tortilla — the Spanish omelette made with potato and onion, rich with eggs and the flavour of good-quality olive oil. Later on we were introduced to Italian frittatas, which are made similarly but can include any delicious tender vegetable — zucchini, artichoke or capsicum — the possibilities are endless.

I often make frittata with the fresh eggs and young vegetables that I have bought after a visit to my local growers market. Everyone seems to like them and they are not only good for you but also very easy to make. This is one of my favourite frittata combinations of asparagus and prosciutto and it is just as good cold as it is hot!

1 bunch asparagus or 300 g baby zucchini
2 tablespoons olive oil
12 large eggs
½ cup grated parmesan cheese
freshly ground black pepper
a little freshly chopped oregano or marjoram
125 g sliced prosciutto, cut into large squares

SERVES 6

Break the tough ends from the asparagus stalks and wash stalks thoroughly. If using baby zucchini, leave them whole, just trimming the stem ends. Larger ones should be cut in halves or quarters lengthwise. Heat 1 tablespoon of the oil in a large frying pan (about 23–25 cm) and gently pan-fry the asparagus or zucchini for about 3 minutes until softened and bright green. Add ½ cup of water and cook another 2 minutes until tender. Remove from pan and set aside.

Meanwhile, lightly beat the eggs in a bowl and add the parmesan, pepper, oregano or marjoram, and prosciutto. Reheat the pan with the remaining oil and pour in the egg mixture. Cook over a moderate heat for 2 minutes and arrange the asparagus or zucchini decoratively on the eggs. Continue cooking until partially set, then run a spatula around the edges to separate the frittata from the pan.

Place a plate on top and invert the pan. Slip the uncooked side back into the pan to cook until golden. Alternatively, instead of inverting the frittata, place the pan underneath a hot griller until an even, light golden brown. Cut into wedges to serve.

Crab Cakes

Many years ago in New York, my partner Mike and I discovered a new seafood restaurant. I ordered Maine lobster, which I had read about, while Mike — who didn't like fish with bones or seafood with shells — ordered crab cakes. He enjoyed them so much that the next time we went back I ordered crab cakes, and from that moment I was hooked. The restaurant gave me the recipe.

Back home I bought blue swimmer crabs and picked out the crabmeat to make these cakes. It was labour intensive! Then during a holiday in the Myall Lakes in New South Wales, I discovered a fish co-op where there was a crew picking out crabmeat with hairpins, which they supplied to restaurants. Now it is often available at fish markets, sometimes frozen — but make sure you get the real thing. This New York recipe is unusual, but the mayonnaise and baking powder are essential. The baking powder seems to crisp the edges and makes the crab cakes light.

2 thick slices bread, crusts removed
milk to cover
500 g picked-over crabmeat
1 tablespoon good-quality mayonnaise
½ teaspoon salt
1 tablespoon Worcestershire sauce
1½ teaspoons baking powder
1 tablespoon chopped flat-leaf parsley
seasoned flour for light coating
light olive or rice bran oil for frying
lemon wedges for serving

SERVES 4

Soak the bread in enough milk to cover for 15 minutes. Gently squeeze out excess milk and place bread in a bowl with the crabmeat, mayonnaise, salt, Worcestershire sauce, baking powder and parsley. Work into a combined mixture. With slightly wet hands shape the mixture into 8–10 patties, dust with flour and fry in oil on each side until golden. Drain on paper towels and serve as soon as possible with lemon wedges. You can serve these patties with a green salad to make them a meal.

NOTE - The patties can be made in miniature for cocktail-size crab cakes.

Salt and Pepper Calamari

Calamari are prized for their sweet, tender flesh and can be bought fresh and ready-cleaned, or frozen. You can freeze them yourself too, with little loss of flavour and texture. Calamari need very light cooking otherwise they become tough.

This simple recipe is best made in a wok as you use less oil. The important thing is to have family and friends sitting and waiting for this crispy delight as it is best eaten piping hot.

500 g calamari tubes
1 cup plain flour
½ teaspoon sea salt
2–4 cups rice bran or light olive oil for
  deep-frying
sea salt and freshly ground black pepper
3 cups rocket leaves, washed and dried
lemon wedges for serving

SERVES 4

Cut across the calamari tubes to create thin rings. Dry thoroughly using paper towels. Place the flour in a large bowl and season with sea salt. Toss the calamari rings thoroughly in the flour and remove, shaking off excess flour. Set aside.

Heat the oil in a wok or a deep frying pan and fry the calamari rings in several batches until they begin to turn golden brown. Remove with a slotted spoon or tongs and drain on paper towels. Season immediately with sea salt and plenty of pepper and serve on a bed of rocket. Accompany with lemon wedges.

TIP ~ When freezing calamari, wrap tubes individually. If using frozen calamari for this recipe, take them out and thaw them only slightly so they are still solid enough to cut into very thin rings. This thinness makes all the difference.

Chinese Steamed Scallops

Some 20 years ago, while having a family birthday celebration at our favourite Chinese restaurant, we ordered the steamed scallops special. We were truly surprised and delighted when they came in their pretty shells, garnished with fragrant aromatic vegetables, cut needle-thin. Back then, scallops were mostly bought without their shells, which look like the classic shell shape as seen in Botticelli's *Birth of Venus*. These days, most fish markets sell fresh scallops in their shells but if they're not available, arrange 4–5 scallops each in 4 small buttered ramekins and cook in the following way. Don't discard the orange coral, if they have them, as this adds flavour as well as colour to the finished dish.

250 g baby spinach leaves
12 scallops, in shells
6–8 spring onions, cut into matchsticks
6 slices fresh ginger, shredded
¼ cup fresh coriander sprigs
4 teaspoons light soy sauce
2 tablespoons peanut oil
2 teaspoons sesame oil

SERVES 3–4

Wash the spinach leaves. Shake the excess water off the leaves, drop them in a saucepan and cook over a low heat, covered, until wilted. Drain well.

Remove scallops from their shells. Spoon small, equal amounts of the cooked spinach on each of the shells, then top with a scallop. Arrange the shells on a rack in a steamer (a large bamboo steamer is ideal, or use a cake rack in a wok). Scatter half the spring onions and ginger over the scallops, reserving the rest for garnish.

Cover well with aluminium foil or a lid and cook gently over a moderate heat until ready, about 5 minutes. Remove and place the shells on a heated serving dish. Garnish the scallops with the reserved spring onions, ginger and the coriander sprigs. Heat the soy sauce, peanut and sesame oils in a small saucepan, pour over the scallops and serve immediately.

Singapore Noodles

Anyone who has visited Singapore will have tasted this famous noodle dish, often prepared in minutes by a street hawker. Our good friend Onn Ho gave us his family recipe, which he has been making since he was a boy in Malaysia. His tips are particularly useful, especially for the novice.

Onn mixes the curry powder with a little water to create a paste, as dry curry powder fried in hot oil burns very quickly and can be bitter. He likes to use a Malaysian curry powder and says that he usually measures one teaspoon per person.

Onn recommends not draining the noodles; instead, when it is time to add them to the wok, scoop them out of the water with your hands. He adds that if they are too dry, they will break up into little pieces as you try to stir-fry them. While frying the noodles, Onn has half a cup of water ready. He sprinkles the noodles intermittently to prevent them from drying too much and breaking up.

300 g rice vermicelli
½ cup vegetable oil
250 g green (raw) prawns, shelled and deveined
1 medium onion, chopped
1 red capsicum, cut into fine strips
2 eggs, lightly beaten
4–6 teaspoons hot curry powder
2 cups bean sprouts
3 tablespoons light soy sauce
salt and freshly ground black pepper
1 tablespoon sesame oil
sprigs of coriander, to garnish

SERVES 4–6

In a large bowl, soak the vermicelli in enough cold water to cover for 15 minutes. Meanwhile, heat 1 tablespoon of the oil in a wok or very large frying pan until hot without smoking. Stir-fry the prawns for 1 minute until they turn pink. Remove and set aside. Heat 2 tablespoons of the oil in the wok and stir-fry the onion and capsicum for 1 minute. Remove and set aside with the prawns.

Add the beaten eggs to the wok and cook in a sheet, rather like an omelette. Remove and cut into thin slices before setting aside.

Add the remaining oil to the wok, stir in the curry powder mixed to a paste with a little water, and the noodles, which have been scooped from the water and drained. Stir-fry until thoroughly combined. Add the prawns, onion and capsicum mixture, omelette strips and bean sprouts, seasoning the mixture with soy sauce and salt and pepper. Stir-fry for 4–5 minutes until the noodles are just cooked. Transfer to a serving platter, drizzle with sesame oil and garnish with coriander.

Crispy Fried Whitebait

A few years ago a group of chefs, food writers and good cooks who had recently returned from Greece as guests of the International Olive Oil Council gathered for a reunion on the deck of my harbourside home.

Originally from Greece, the acclaimed chef Janni Kyritsis' eyes brightened when he saw the fresh whitebait I had found on my morning visit to the fish markets. He tossed them in seasoned flour and fried them in olive oil for a minute or two until they were golden and crispy. He then gave someone the job of salting and peppering them as the batches were done, and giving each a squeeze of lemon. Serve them as a first course or an appetiser with drinks.

light olive oil or rice bran oil for deep-frying
500 g whitebait or small anchovies
  (3–5 cm long)
4 tablespoons plain flour, seasoned with salt
  and freshly ground black pepper
sea salt and freshly ground black pepper
lemon wedges

SERVES 4–6

Fill a wok to one-third with the oil and heat until almost smoking. Lightly dust fish with seasoned flour and fry in batches for about 2 minutes each, turning constantly in the oil. Remove each batch with a slotted spoon and drain on paper towels. If needed, add more oil to the wok as you continue frying the fish.

When all are cooked, repeat the frying process for a couple of seconds at a time and drain on fresh paper towels. Twice-frying is the secret of a crisp finish. When they are all done, season with sea salt and pepper, squeeze with lemon juice and serve immediately.

NOTE ~ Whitebait are tiny, very young fish. In New Zealand, whitebait are particularly small, tender and sweet, and are mostly used in fritters and omelettes. This type of whitebait is too small to prepare as described above because the fish stay in a mass and can't be cooked separately. The fish I am referring to can be called silver fish or whitebait. They are 3–5 cm long and look like very small sardines.

Kedgeree

The recipe for kedgeree was brought back from India by serving British regiment officers in Victorian times. The British colonists living in India came under the spell of rice and spices, and added their 'finnan haddies', or smoked haddock, to a traditional Indian dish called kitchri.

Kedgeree was one of the simple family dishes that my mother would cook for me and my five siblings. She made it with Scotch haddock, which is hard to find today, so I like to use smoked haddock, a quality canned red salmon or fresh salmon. When kedgeree is cooked carefully it is delicious, so keep an eye on the details.

3 smoked haddock fillets
2 tablespoons oil
1 medium onion, sliced
1 teaspoon curry powder
2 tablespoons sultanas
2 hard-boiled eggs
2–3 tablespoons cream
2 cups cooked long-grain rice (see Tip)
1 cup cooked peas (optional)
a pinch of salt
3 tablespoons chopped coriander
   or flat-leaf parsley
lime or lemon quarters and 30 g butter
   for serving

SERVES 6

Poach the haddock fillets in gently simmering water for 5 minutes. Drain and remove skin and bones. Flake into small pieces and set aside. Heat oil in a wide frying pan over a medium heat and sauté the onion until soft and golden. Stir in the curry powder and sultanas and cook for another minute or so.

Stir in the flaked fish, one of the eggs (roughly chopped), cream, rice, peas (if using) and salt to taste. Reheat gently, tossing with a fork. Turn onto a serving dish and scatter with chopped coriander or parsley and the remaining egg, sliced or quartered. Serve with lime or lemon quarters and top with the lump of butter. Serve piping hot.

TIP ~ To cook the rice, measure ¾ cup of long-grain rice. Wash well with several changes of water. Bring 1½ cups of water to the boil in a medium saucepan with ½ teaspoon of salt, then add rice. Allow the water to return to the boil, stir once, and cover with a well-fitting lid. Turn the heat down as low as possible and cook gently for 20 minutes. Remove from the heat and uncover for a few minutes to allow the steam to escape. Fluff up the rice with a fork. Makes 2 cups.

Indian Ghee Rice

The recipe for Indian ghee rice was in my very first cookbook and it was while I was writing it and Suzanne was doing much of the shopping and housework back home that she put it to the test. She had no official training up until then apart from standing beside me as she grew up, stirring, preparing lamb chops for grilling, slicing tomatoes for salads, and watching. She was so delighted at her success with the Indian ghee rice that she changed her mind (as 18-year-olds are inclined to do) about becoming a fashion designer and gave in to pursuing a career in food. With the help of my first royalty cheque I was able to send her off to London to complete the Cordon Bleu Diploma Course. The rest, as they say, is history.

The easiest and most successful way to cook rice is by the absorption method. The rice is first fried in ghee, and then simmered in stock and spices until all the liquid has evaporated, and the rice has become tender, but with each grain still separate. Do not stir rice once it has come to the boil.

60 g ghee or butter
1 onion, finely sliced
1 teaspoon ground turmeric
2 cups basmati rice
3½ cups hot Chicken Stock (page 237)
   or water
8 black peppercorns
2 whole cloves
4 bruised cardamom pods
1 stick cinnamon
2 teaspoons salt
1 cup cooked peas

SERVES 4–6

Heat the ghee or butter in a heavy saucepan with a lid. Add the onion to the pan and fry gently until a golden brown. Make sure the onion is well cooked, but do not allow it to burn. This frying takes quite a while. Add the turmeric and cook, stirring, for 1 minute. Add the rice and fry for 5–10 minutes, stirring constantly, until it is golden. Add hot stock or water with the spices and salt. When boiling, turn the heat down very low, cover the pan tightly and cook gently for 20–25 minutes. Add the peas in the last 10 minutes of cooking. Turn the heat off and keep covered until ready to serve.

A few minutes before serving, uncover the pan to allow steam to escape. Fluff up the rice with a fork. >>

Indian ghee rice with chicken

To turn the rice into a complete meal in 1 pan you can add 4 chicken thigh or breast fillets, cut in two.

In a large heavy frying pan, brown the chicken pieces on all sides in the ghee, then set aside. Add the onion to the pan and fry until golden brown, stirring well for 1 minute. Add the turmeric and rice and fry for a few minutes, stirring until golden. Add the hot stock and spices. Season with salt to taste. Return the chicken to the pan, pushing it down into the rice.

Cover with a tight-fitting lid and cook on a very low heat for 15 minutes. Add the peas and continue to cook until the chicken is tender and the rice has absorbed the liquid. A few minutes before serving, uncover, and fluff up the rice with a fork.

WHAT IS GHEE?

Ghee is a clarified butter essential to many Indian dishes. It is made by gently simmering unsalted butter until its water content is removed. The resulting butter is spooned off leaving white milk solids, which settle to the bottom. The white milk solids should be discarded. Ghee has a delicious nutty aroma and is able to be heated to higher temperatures than normal butter without burning. You can also purchase ghee from the supermarket.

Risotto alla Milanese

This creamy, luxurious dish, when made with good Italian risotto rice and homemade chicken stock, is food for the gods. Risotto can be as simple as rice, stock and parmesan or can be richly studded with seafood, vegetables or even bone marrow. The slow-cooking method results in a creamy texture with each grain separate and still firm to the bite. The liquid is added slowly and the rice is stirred constantly. It takes 20–25 minutes, but it is worth every minute.

Risotto should be made with arborio, carnaroli, vialone nano, roma or baldo rice, most of which are grown along the Po River Valley in Italy's north and are available in many Italian delis or supermarkets. These rice varieties are able to absorb liquid and stand up to long, slow cooking without becoming soft and mushy.

6 cups Chicken Stock (page 237)
a large pinch of saffron threads
2 tablespoons olive oil
30 g butter
1 onion, finely diced
1½ cups arborio, carnaroli or vialone rice
extra butter (optional)
2 tablespoons grated parmesan cheese
salt and freshly ground black pepper

SERVES 4–6

Bring the chicken stock to a simmer and keep hot. Add the pinch of saffron. Heat the oil and butter in a heavy-based saucepan and fry the onion gently until golden. Add the rice and stir with a wooden spoon until glistening.

Add a ladleful of stock, stirring constantly. When the stock has been absorbed, add another ladle, stirring, until almost all the stock is added and the rice is tender, 20–25 minutes. If necessary, add boiling water to the rice to complete cooking. At this stage remove the saucepan from the heat and without stirring add enough remaining stock to give the risotto a creamy consistency. Some cooks like to cover the saucepan with a lid and leave it to stand for 5–10 minutes before serving.

Just before serving, add a nut of butter, if you like, plus the grated cheese, stirring both into the rice. Season with salt and pepper and serve.

TIP ~ Cook risotto in a heavy-based saucepan, preferably with a rounded base to prevent the rice from sticking. It needs to be big enough to accommodate the rice, which will swell to as much as three times its original size. The stock must be kept gently simmering, to prevent the cooking process slowing down. Saffron is an essential ingredient.

Parisian Gnocchi

Three happy years of my life were spent training at the East Sydney Hotel and Restaurant Cookery School. There, I was introduced to international and, in particular, French cooking as dictated by Escoffier, the master of French cuisine.

One of the great joys was learning about dishes that can be made with choux pastry. Not only can it be used to make profiteroles and éclairs, it can form the base for many savoury dishes like gougères and gnocchi.

Parisian gnocchi, also known as gnocchi fondenti, is a dish typical of the Emilia-Romagna region in Italy. The Italian 'fondenti' literally translates as 'melt-in-your-mouth'.

1½ cups plain flour
1½ cups water
75 g butter, cut into small pieces
½ teaspoon salt
a good pinch of ground nutmeg
3 eggs
½ cup grated parmesan cheese
1½ cups cream
3 tablespoons grated gruyère or other
　Swiss-style cheese
a pinch of ground cayenne

SERVES 6-8

Sift the flour onto a piece of greaseproof paper and set aside. Heat the water in a heavy saucepan with the butter, salt and nutmeg. When boiling and once the butter has melted, pour in the flour, stirring rapidly. When the mixture begins to form a ball remove from heat and cool. Beat in the eggs, one at a time. When the mixture is smooth and shiny beat in half the grated parmesan.

Bring a large pan of salted water to a gentle simmer and place a rack topped with a tea towel next to it. Use 2 tablespoons to scoop, shape and drop tablespoon measures of mixture into gently simmering water in batches. Cook for about 5 minutes, until they rise to the surface. Lift out with a slotted spoon and arrange on the towel-topped rack. This amount should be cooked in three batches. Gnocchi can be prepared to this stage several hours ahead, or even the night before. Store in the refrigerator, covered.

Preheat the oven to 200°C (400°F). Cover the base of two large, shallow ovenproof dishes with ½ cup of the cream and arrange the cooked gnocchi on top in a layer. Heat the remaining cream with the remaining grated parmesan and Swiss-style cheese and spoon over the gnocchi. Sprinkle over the cayenne and bake for about 15 minutes, until gnocchi have puffed, the sauce is bubbling and the top is golden.

Ricotta Gnocchi with Fresh Tomato Sauce

I love traditional potato gnocchi and have enjoyed it in Italian homes and restaurants, but for some reason I've never had much success making it myself. A good Italian friend came to my rescue with this recipe, which uses low-fat ricotta instead of potato and — presto — it worked, so now I can enjoy gnocchi whenever I like.

250 g low-fat ricotta
⅓ cup grated parmesan cheese
1 large egg
1 teaspoon salt
1 cup plain flour
shaved parmesan cheese

TOMATO SAUCE
1 teaspoon olive oil
2 cloves garlic, finely chopped
1 punnet cherry tomatoes, quartered
6 basil leaves, chopped

SERVES 4

Combine the ricotta, grated parmesan, egg and salt in a bowl. Add the flour and mix. Add only as much flour as you need to create a workable dough, and be careful not to overwork it. Divide the dough into four, and roll each piece into a 2 cm-thick log. Cut into 2 cm slices and gently place on a lightly floured baking sheet. Press down with the back of a fork to make indents in each gnocchi. Continue with the remaining dough in this manner. If not using immediately, chill.

To prepare the sauce, heat the oil and add the garlic, cooking only until fragrant. Do not brown. Add the tomatoes and basil and bring to the boil, then reduce to low and simmer for 8 minutes.

To cook the gnocchi, drop them in several batches into a saucepan of simmering, lightly salted water and remove as soon as they float to the top, after 1 or 2 minutes. Place in a warmed bowl, top with some tomato sauce and gently mix. Scatter over some parmesan.

TIP - The secret to making these gnocchi is to dry the ingredients as much as you can before using. Drain excess water from ricotta by placing it in a colander over a bowl and leaving it in the refrigerator for at least 30 minutes.

Spaghetti all'Amatriciana

Spaghetti all'Amatriciana comes from Amatrice, a little village in the Apennine Mountains, near Rome. Tubular strands of bucatini are the best pasta for this tomato, pancetta and chilli sauce — they're perfectly designed to take on the delicious flavours.

There's some debate over whether onion should be included; it seems in Amatrice that it is not. There's also discussion about whether to leave the chilli whole and remove it, or finely chop it to make the sauce hotter. I think this is entirely up to you!

¼ cup olive oil
1 onion, thinly sliced
150 g pancetta or bacon, cut into strips
½ cup dry white wine
4 medium tomatoes, peeled, seeded and
  chopped, or 1 x 400 g can chopped tomatoes
1 small dried or birdseye chilli
salt and freshly ground black pepper
a pinch of cayenne
375 g spaghetti or bucatini
¼ cup grated parmesan cheese
2 tablespoons grated pecorino cheese

SERVES 4

Heat the olive oil in a frying pan and sauté the onion over a gentle heat until soft. Add the pancetta or bacon and fry slowly for a few minutes. Moisten with wine and continue cooking until it evaporates a little.

Add the tomatoes to the pan with the chilli. If using canned tomatoes, try to flick out the seeds before adding with a little of the tomato juice. Season to taste with salt, pepper and cayenne and cook over a brisk heat for 15 minutes. Remove the chilli.

Bring a large saucepan of salted water to the boil. Lower the pasta into the water, stir well and cook for 10–12 minutes or until al dente (tender to the bite). Drain and toss the pasta with the tomato sauce. Sprinkle grated parmesan and pecorino on top.

Spaghetti alla Carbonara

Giving credit where it is due is important in most families — particularly when it comes to cooking. My niece, a very good cook herself, stayed with a family in Italy who introduced her to spaghetti alla carbonara.

Uncle was heralded the best carbonara cook. He was very particular about the small details and would squeeze the butter between his fingers to break it up and get it soft. He was fussy about the quality of pancetta — Italy's answer to bacon — and was also particular about parmesan cheese, which is an inseparable part of Italian cooking, often tasting it before he bought it. Good parmesan is aged for three to four years, sometimes even longer, and has no peer for grating over pasta.

I have been making this dish for years, and even though I follow all the rules I can't quite get it to Uncle's standard — it's still good, though, and well worth trying.

500 g spaghetti
3 eggs
½ cup cream
200 g pancetta or bacon, rind removed
60 g butter
⅓ cup chopped flat-leaf parsley
about ½ cup grated parmesan cheese
freshly ground black pepper

SERVES 4

Cook the spaghetti in a large pan of boiling salted water for about 15 minutes or until tender but still firm. Drain and turn into a heated serving bowl, covering to keep the pasta warm. Beat the eggs lightly with the cream and set aside. Meanwhile, cut the pancetta or bacon into thin strips and cook gently in a pan in a little of the butter for a few minutes or until crispy.

Just before serving, stir the eggs into the pancetta and cook over a very gentle heat until the eggs just start to thicken. Pour onto the spaghetti, tossing well with the remaining butter (the idea is that the butter has been softened and should stay creamy, not quite melting, which would make it oily) and chopped parsley. Add the parmesan, season well with pepper and toss again.

NOTE ~ Pancetta is the fat and lean meat cut only from the belly of the pig, and is cured with salt, pepper and other spices without being smoked. It is tightly rolled into a sausage and sold in pieces or sliced. When it is good quality, it can be eaten just like ham or prosciutto.

Spaghetti Bolognese

Bologna is lovingly referred to as the cradle of Italian cooking. It is said that this Bolognese dish was devised in 1487 on the occasion of the marriage of Lucrezia Borgia. The cook, inspired by the bride's beautiful hair, made it using tagliatelle — a ribbon-like pasta — paired with the rich sauce or ragù of the region.

I cannot help admiring the Italian enjoyment of food and nowhere is it more apparent than in Bologna. I remember seeing a rotund diner at his usual restaurant, at his usual table, tucking a huge snowy napkin under his collar, and in front of him was a steaming bowl of pasta with its Bolognese sauce. He sat alone and I was informed that he had been doing that same thing for 30 years.

500 g–1 kg spaghetti (see Tip)
½–1 quantity Bolognese Sauce (opposite)
grated parmesan cheese

SERVES 4–8

Use a large saucepan with plenty of room for the pasta to cook evenly and not stick together. For every 250 g of pasta use 14 cups of water seasoned with 1 teaspoon of salt. Boil the water vigorously before adding the pasta. Do not add oil at this point — although it helps stop the pasta sticking together it also prevents the sauce from clinging to the pasta. In any case, only inferior pasta is inclined to stick together, so use a quality brand.

Lower the spaghetti slowly into the saucepan so that the water stays on the boil. Stir a few times to start and then leave to boil vigorously. Cooked pasta should be tender but still firm — 'al dente' as the Italians say. When cooked, remove immediately from the heat and drain the pasta, reserving 1 or 2 tablespoons of the cooking water. Do not rinse, as the sauce will not cling so readily to rinsed pasta.

Add the Bolognese sauce to the cooked spaghetti and toss over a gentle heat for 1 minute, adding some of the parmesan at this point. If the pasta seems dry, add a little of the reserved cooking water. Sprinkle with more parmesan and serve.

TIP ~ While Bolognese sauce is often teamed with spaghetti, it can also be eaten with other types of pasta such as tagliatelle, rigatoni, or even gnocchi.

Bolognese Sauce

Also called 'ragù' or 'sugo alla Bolognese', it is said that there are as many recipe versions of this delicious slow-cooked sauce as there are cooks in the Italian city of Bologna. The Bolognese claim that a true ragù cannot be made anywhere else. Perhaps this is so but, if you follow a few rules, the following recipe is very good without taking four hours to cook, as is suggested by some recipes.

Use a deep, heavy-based saucepan and keep the heat as low as possible while the sauce is simmering. Use lean beef, preferably finely chopped chuck steak, rather than mince. Cream is added to soften the sauce, but some cooks prefer adding a little butter.

1 tablespoon olive oil
2 medium onions, finely diced
2 celery stalks, finely sliced
1 large carrot, finely diced
150 g pancetta, chopped
1 clove garlic, crushed
1 kg chuck steak, trimmed and finely chopped
1 cup dry white or red wine
2 x 400 g cans chopped tomatoes
¼ cup cream or a little butter (optional)
a pinch of ground nutmeg
salt and freshly ground black pepper

SERVES 8

Heat the oil in a large, heavy-based saucepan over a medium heat. Sauté the onions for 3–5 minutes, without colouring. Add the celery, carrot, pancetta and garlic and continue to cook for another 5 minutes, until the vegetables are soft.

Increase the heat to high. Add the steak and cook for 4 minutes, until the colour changes. Add the wine and bring to the boil. Stir in the tomatoes, reduce heat to low and simmer, covered, for 1½–2 hours.

Remove the lid and simmer for another 20 minutes, until the sauce thickens and the meat is tender. Stir in the cream or butter, if using, and nutmeg. Season to taste with salt and a good grinding of pepper.

TIP - Bolognese sauce is best made the day before to allow the flavours to develop. After cooking, cool quickly and refrigerate in an airtight container.

Main Meals

Paella Valenciana

Paella is one of the glories of Spanish cuisine: deliciously flavoured and golden with saffron-infused rice, morsels of meat, seafood and vegetables. I first learnt to make paella from a Spanish-Mexican friend whose practice was to have all the ingredients ready in bowls and plates before cooking — what the French call *mise en place*.

With the outdoor barbecue lit and the paella pan set on the hot coals, the ritual could begin. The chicken was cooked in Spanish olive oil, then the onions, rice and so on, while we nibbled on Spanish olives and chorizo, sipping wine and admiring the skills of our host. The trick is to gently cook the paella without burning the bottom. A watchful and loving eye is essential, to move the pan around and add more stock as needed. My friend taught us how to arrange the foods attractively on the rice. At last, the paella was placed in the centre of the table and everyone helped themselves, sometimes offering little tidbits to a neighbouring guest. It was all very informal and great fun.

½ teaspoon saffron threads

5 cups Chicken Stock (page 237)

½ cup olive oil

4 large chicken pieces such as half-breast or thigh fillets

1 red capsicum, sliced into strips

2 onions, chopped

2 cloves garlic, chopped

2½ cups medium shortgrain rice such as calasparra or arborio

6 or 7 anchovy fillets

2 tomatoes, peeled and sliced, each half into 6 wedges

1 cup shelled green peas

500 g fresh, uncooked seafood such as scallops, prawns, calamari or mussels (see overleaf)

SERVES 6–8

Prepare all ingredients and arrange them on a tray. Bring the saffron and stock to the boil, and set aside until ready to use. Heat the oil in a large paella pan or wide, deep frying pan. You may have to straddle the pan over two burners on the stove if you are cooking indoors. Sauté the chicken pieces until golden. Remove and cut into three, removing any small bones. Set aside. Add the capsicum to the pan, cook for a few minutes, then remove and set aside.

Add the onions and garlic to the pan and cook until soft. Add the rice and fry gently for 3–4 minutes, then add the stock. When the rice is bubbling, reduce the heat and start the decoration of the paella. Add the chicken, capsicum, anchovy fillets, tomatoes, green peas and seafood in a pattern around the dish. The idea is to add the seafood in the order it takes to cook. Add more stock if necessary and simmer gently until the rice is done, 20–25 minutes.

Allow 2–3 pieces of each small shellfish per person, and prepare as follows. >>

Green (raw) prawns

These are best left whole; that is, heads, shells and tails still on. However, they may also be shelled, the heads removed, and a cut made down the back to remove the intestinal tract.

Calamari or baby squid

Gently pull the tentacles from the hood (pocket-like part) of the squid, then hold under running water to rinse away any ink. Pull out the hard material that forms the skeleton. Slice squid into rings. Cut away the hard 'beak' from the tentacles.

Mussels or pipis

Scrub mussels well using a good stiff brush. Pull off the beard that clings around the edges. Soak mussels or pipis in cold water — they should disgorge any sand. Discard any that are not shut tightly.

Scallops

Remove brown bits from the main scallop muscle, then rinse scallops in fresh water. Corals may be used.

NOTE ~ Pork can replace the chicken. Use 3–4 pork chops and cook as for chicken.

Good kitchen shops sell paella pans. They come in a variety of sizes, ranging from small (for four serves) to large (for up to 20 people). Otherwise, use a wide, deep frying pan or baking dish.

Salmon and Eggplant Curry

Forty years ago I visited Thailand and was entertained by a member of the Thai royal family. She ran her own cooking school and was one of the first people to can the spicy curry sauces and pastes that can be so time-consuming to make. I brought back some of her canned goods, which were quite a novelty at the time.

The advent of bottled exotic pastes, sauces and coconut milk, plus fresh South-East Asian ingredients, has since delighted us all, and opened our minds and tastebuds to new flavour combinations.

The salmon is a bit of a surprise in this recipe, but it goes very well with the strong Thai spices. It is rich, though, so if you prefer use coconut milk in place of the coconut cream for a lighter result. If you can't find baby eggplants use one medium eggplant, cut into long, thin strips.

½ cup peanut or rice bran oil for frying
6 baby (Lebanese) eggplants, trimmed and cut in half lengthwise
1 cup coconut cream or milk
2 fresh kaffir lime leaves, finely chopped, plus extra to garnish
2 tablespoons green curry paste
4 salmon steaks, skinned and each cut into 4 strips widthwise
lime wedges for serving

SERVES 6–8

Heat half the oil in a frying pan over a high heat. Cook the eggplant pieces in batches for 2–3 minutes on each side, until golden brown, adding more oil if necessary. Set aside on paper towels to drain.

Combine the coconut cream or milk, lime leaves and curry paste in a saucepan over a medium heat. Stir until boiling, reduce heat and simmer for 5 minutes.

Cook the salmon strips in the coconut sauce in batches for 1 minute on each side. Transfer to a serving bowl. Add the eggplant pieces to the sauce, stir to coat and simmer for 2 minutes to heat through.

Spoon the eggplant and sauce over the salmon and top with extra lime leaves. Serve with lime wedges and steamed rice.

Fish à la Meunière

I am lucky that I live five minutes away from one of the best fish markets in the world. No, not the Fulton Fish Market of New York, but the fish market in Sydney's Pyrmont.

I'm very fussy when it comes to fish. It's important not to overcook it and to resist the temptation to swamp it with sauces and flavourings. Fish has such a wonderful natural flavour.

This dish translates from the French as 'in the style of the miller's wife', who presumably must have had fish swimming in her mill pond. The gentle method of à la meunière, it has been said, is the perfect way to cook delicate fish, the classic French choice being sole. You could also use John Dory, flathead tails, whiting fillets, snapper or bream fillets. Whole trout can also be cooked à la meunière. Very little else is needed, except perhaps potatoes that have been steamed and lightly buttered, and a green salad on the side.

about ½ cup plain flour, seasoned with
   sea salt and freshly ground black pepper
4 fish fillets (185–200 g), skinned
60 g butter
1 tablespoon light olive oil
juice of 1 lemon
1 tablespoon chopped flat-leaf parsley
lemon wedges for serving

SERVES 4

Put the seasoned flour in a shallow bowl and dust the fish lightly. Melt a tablespoon of the butter with the oil in a large frying pan over a medium heat. Add the fish and first cook one side to a delicate brown for 2–3 minutes, then turn and cook the other side. Arrange on a serving plate and keep warm. Return the frying pan to low heat, add the remaining butter and cook until it has a golden brown colour and a nutty aroma. Add the lemon juice, swirl until combined and then add the chopped parsley. Pour immediately over the fish and serve at once with lemon wedges.

Fish amandine

After the fish is cooked and set aside, add ¼ cup of slivered or halved blanched almonds to the butter in the pan. Cook until almonds are golden, stirring frequently. Pour over the fish and drizzle with lemon juice.

Fish Stew with Rouille Sauce

I first tried a fish stew in Marseilles many years ago, when I was introduced to bouillabaisse — the famous dish originally made by fishermen from the Mediterranean. Some fishermen are good cooks and each coastal fishing village has their own way of preparing dishes from a mixed catch. Fish is important to our daily diet and therefore I highly recommend this simple fish stew. However, take care — fish may be easy to cook, but it is also easy to spoil if you overcook it.

2 tablespoons olive oil
1 small onion, finely diced
1 celery stalk or ½ fennel bulb, chopped
3 cloves garlic, crushed
a large pinch of saffron threads
4 ripe tomatoes, diced
2 cups water
¾ cup dry white wine
salt and freshly ground black pepper
1.5 kg fresh, uncooked seafood such as fish
  cutlets and fillets, mussels, prawns or scallops
  (see page 84 for preparation)
a little lemon juice
freshly chopped flat-leaf parsley, to garnish

ROUILLE SAUCE
2 cloves garlic, crushed
½ cup pimientos, well drained
2 egg yolks
a pinch of saffron threads
¾ cup olive oil

SERVES 4

Heat the oil in a heavy-based pan and sauté the onion gently until soft, about 5 minutes. Add the celery or fennel, garlic and saffron, stir for a minute and add the tomatoes. Cook, stirring, until thick and pulpy. Add the water, wine, salt and pepper to taste and simmer gently for about 10 minutes.

Add the prepared seafood and cook gently. When the fish is tender and whitened, the prawns pink and the mussels opened, the seafood is cooked. Taste and add more seasoning if necessary. A little lemon juice to taste can be squeezed over at this point.

To make the rouille sauce, add the garlic, pimientos, egg yolks and saffron to a blender or food processor. Purée until smooth, and then with the machine running add the olive oil, drop by drop at first, then more quickly as the sauce thickens.

To serve, ladle the stew into 4 bowls and garnish with chopped parsley. Have a basket of crusty bread on the table and hand around the bowl of rouille for each guest to add a spoonful to their stew as desired.

Steamed Fish Coriander

On my first trip to China in 1976 I visited Mao's birthplace. We were taken to communes to see how Chinese people lived, ate, dressed and were schooled. I had been told before I left not to expect great food as the Chinese ate very simply. In fact, as I discovered, they ate very well. On a visit to one commune we were shown a lake where fish swam. The cadre gave the signal for fish to be caught and in what seemed like minutes we were sitting down to beautiful fish smothered with the finest aromatic vegetables. The Chinese are masters at cooking fish and balancing the seasonings, as this dish shows.

The fish is steamed almost to the point of being cooked, and then placed on a warm platter and seasoned. Hot, smoking oil is poured over just before it is taken to the table, which finishes the cooking and makes the flavour of the aromatic herbs and vegetables permeate the fish. The garnish of shredded spring onions, coriander and ginger is fantastic!

1 whole fish (about 1.5 kg) such as jewfish, snapper, barramundi or coral trout, scaled and cleaned
salt
3 spring onions, sliced
4 slices fresh ginger
roots and stems of ½ bunch fresh coriander
1 cup water

GARNISH
4 spring onions, finely shredded
6 slices fresh ginger, finely shredded
½ cup fresh coriander leaves
2 tablespoons peanut or rice bran oil
2 teaspoons sesame oil
1 tablespoon light soy sauce

SERVES 6

Score the fish with three diagonal cuts on each side of the thickest part and lightly salt inside and out. Place half the spring onions, ginger and coriander roots and stems in the cavity of the fish. Lay the remaining onions, ginger and coriander on a rack in the bottom of a flameproof dish to form a bed for the fish. Put the fish on top and add the water. Cover with foil or a lid and cook gently, for 10–15 minutes. You will know if the fish is cooked by the eyes, which should be white when it is done. To be sure, use a sharp pointed knife to make a small cut along a section of the backbone to see if the flesh lifts easily away from the bone.

Place the fish on a heated serving dish and garnish with the shredded spring onions, ginger and coriander leaves. Heat the peanut and sesame oils in a small pan, then pour over the fish (if the oil is hot enough there should be lots of sizzling). Sprinkle with soy sauce and serve immediately with steamed rice.

Chinese White Chicken

I visited China four days after Chairman Mao died. One fifth of the world's population was in mourning, but as a visitor I was not expected to grieve. Instead my host treated me to many special dishes.

It was fascinating to learn new cooking techniques, especially the method used for white chicken. I was encouraged to chew the bones and enjoy their special flavour. In return, I was asked to show my hosts how to make a chicken sandwich, which they proceeded to eat with chopsticks! Life is full of surprises.

When cooking this dish, don't be alarmed if the chicken flesh gets a slight pearly pink colour and the bones are a little red in the centre. This is how it should be, and it's the way the Chinese love it.

1 size 15 (1.5 kg) chicken
4 spring onions, roughly chopped
2 cm piece fresh ginger, peeled and sliced
1 teaspoon salt
about 12 cups boiling Chicken Stock
   (page 237) or water
1 tablespoon sesame oil
½ cup fresh coriander leaves
2 extra spring onions, thinly shredded
Green Onion Dipping Sauce (opposite)

SERVES 6

Remove any visible fat from the chicken and wipe with paper towels. Place breast-side down in a large heavy-based saucepan, add 4 of the spring onions, the ginger and salt. Add enough boiling water or stock to just cover the chicken and bring to the boil over a medium heat. Reduce heat, cover and simmer for 10 minutes. Remove from the heat and leave the chicken to stand and cool in the liquid for 45 minutes. Drain the cooking liquid and use as stock for other recipes or freeze it.

Prepare a large bowl half-filled with cold water and ice cubes. Remove the chicken from the pan, draining well, particularly any liquid from the cavity. As soon as the chicken is drained, plunge it into the bowl of iced water. Leave for 15 minutes, until cold. Lift the chicken out carefully, drain thoroughly and pat dry with paper towels. Place the chicken on a plate and rub all over with sesame oil. Cover loosely with foil and refrigerate until ready to serve. Using a heavy cleaver, cut the chicken into pieces (see page opposite). Toss together the extra spring onions and coriander leaves and scatter over the chicken. Serve with green onion dipping sauce.

Green Onion Dipping Sauce

4 tablespoons peanut or rice bran oil
1 teaspoon salt
6 spring onions, finely sliced
2 tablespoons finely chopped fresh ginger

MAKES ABOUT ⅓ CUP

Heat the oil in a small saucepan over a high heat and when almost smoking, remove from the heat and carefully add the salt, spring onions and ginger.

TO CHOP A CHICKEN

Place chicken on a strong wooden board and split into halves, using a heavy cleaver. Remove the wing joints (reserving them), then the marylands, chopping each thigh section in three and each drumstick in two. Arrange these pieces on a serving platter. Chop away and discard excess bone from the two breast pieces, then cut each across into 2 cm slices. Arrange on top of the first lot of chicken. Finish with the wings.

French Roast Chicken Dinner

When I was a girl, a roast chicken dinner was a rare treat, enjoyed by our family only once a month. Now we cook chicken in a variety of ways, several times a week, but sometimes I still want roast chicken the way it was — firm to the bite, and tasting so good on its own — you hardly need to do anything but roast it with a little sea salt, pepper and butter or olive oil. I also prefer to have chicken less often and pay a bit extra for a quality organic bird — one that has scratched around and pecked the ground and had some sort of life.

This kind of chicken dinner is worth travelling miles for, especially on a Sunday. The French roasting method is to add stock to the baking dish and baste the chicken during the cooking. The chicken may appear pale but miraculously the skin turns a lovely golden brown towards the end and the flesh stays beautifully moist. The potatoes taste good, too, having taken in some of the flavour of the chicken.

1 size 15–18 (1.5–1.8 kg) free-range chicken
60 g butter or ¼ cup olive oil
salt and freshly ground black pepper
a few tarragon or flat-leaf parsley stalks
3 strips orange rind
1½ cups Chicken Stock (page 237)
500 g baby new potatoes or 4 large desiree
   potatoes, peeled and quartered
½ cup white wine

SERVES 4–6

Preheat the oven to 200°C (400°F). Wipe the cavity of the chicken with a paper towel. Place a little of the butter or oil, the salt, pepper, tarragon or parsley stalks and orange rind inside the chicken cavity.

Truss the chicken (see page 96) and rub all over with the remaining butter or oil. Place the chicken on its side in a baking tray with the stock, preferably on a roasting rack. Add the potatoes to the tray and roast for 20 minutes. Turn the chicken onto the other side, baste with stock and turn the potatoes.

Reduce the oven to 190°C (375°F) and continue to cook for another 50 minutes, turning and basting every 15 minutes and adding more stock (or a little water) when necessary. There should be just enough stock to keep the juices in the pan from scorching. Towards the end of cooking add the wine and turn the chicken on its back for the last 15 minutes to brown the breast. Turn the potatoes from time to time.

To test if the chicken is cooked, run a fine skewer into the thigh joint. The juice should be clear. Remove the chicken from the dish and discard string. Keep in a warm place. >>

Remove the potatoes and keep warm while making gravy (see below), or you can simply deglaze the pan. If the latter, place the baking dish over a medium heat, add 1 cup of stock or white wine and scrape up any bits stuck to the bottom of the pan to mix in with the liquid. Let it bubble and thicken for a few minutes. Pour into a jug and keep warm to serve with the chicken.

You may like to carve some of the breast meat, and then cut the remaining chicken into joints. Arrange on a heated serving dish and surround with the potatoes. Serve with French-style Peas and Vichy Carrots (pages 140, 141), or other young cooked green vegetables, and pan sauce or gravy.

NOTE - To truss a chicken, place chicken on its back, pull the skin over the neck and tuck underneath. Run string across the outside end of the breast, around wings, cross under the back, and then bring back up to tie the legs together, keeping them close to the body. If you want to stuff the chicken, put some of the stuffing into the neck end and some into the body cavity, but don't fill it too tightly. Allow plenty of space for the stuffing to swell and stay light.

If you want to make gravy

Pour off all but 2 tablespoons of the juices from the pan. Add 1 scant tablespoon of flour and stir well until lightly browned. Add 1½ cups of chicken stock and stir until thickened. Season with salt and pepper. Pour into a small saucepan to keep warm or pour into a jug or gravy boat.

Cream gravy

Make gravy as above but just before serving stir in 3 tablespoons of cream and cook a little until thickened.

Mushroom cream gravy

Pour off all but 2 tablespoons of the juices from the pan. Add 8–10 sliced button mushrooms to the pan and cook gently for 3–4 minutes, stirring to cook evenly. Proceed as for gravy, stirring in 3 tablespoons of cream at the end.

Pastitsio

Greeks love food and a party, and I have had the good fortune to have been included in many Greek celebrations — weddings, christenings and Easter festivities. Pastitsio is a great party dish, similar to the Italian lasagne, but uses tubular macaroni instead of flat sheets of pasta. I've borrowed from the Italians by using Bolognese sauce as the base, rather than the minced beef that is usually included in the Greek version. This recipe makes two dishes.

500 g rigatoni
40 g butter, melted
1 cup grated parmesan cheese
salt and freshly ground black pepper
3 eggs, lightly beaten
1 quantity Bolognese Sauce (page 79),
   made without the pancetta

WHITE SAUCE

110 g butter
2/3 cup plain flour
4 cups milk
1/2 teaspoon ground nutmeg
salt and freshly ground black pepper
1 egg, lightly beaten

SERVES 12

Cook the rigatoni in a large saucepan of boiling, salted water according to packet instructions. Drain and return to the pan. Pour over the butter, add half the parmesan and mix well. Season to taste and set aside to cool.

Meanwhile, make the white sauce. Melt the butter in a saucepan over a low heat. Add the flour and cook, stirring, for 2 minutes. Add the milk and bring to the boil, whisking constantly. Cook for 5 minutes, until thickened. Remove from heat, add the nutmeg and season to taste. Cool slightly before whisking in the beaten egg.

Preheat the oven to 200°C (400°F). Grease 2 x 2.5-litre capacity ovenproof dishes. Add the eggs to the pasta and toss to coat. Spoon half of the pasta into the prepared dishes. Cover with Bolognese sauce and top with remaining pasta. Spoon over the white sauce and spread to completely cover the pasta. Sprinkle over the remaining parmesan. Bake for 30 minutes, until golden. Let stand for 10 minutes before serving.

Tandoori Chicken

When on a visit to Kashmir in northern India, my friends and I came upon a group of holidaymakers from Bombay. They were travelling with their own cook, who had a portable tandoor oven. Most days he would make naan bread: the dough would be rolled into balls, flattened by hand and then slapped onto the walls of the hot tandoor. The naan was ready when it bubbled and blistered. Meats and poultry on long skewers were also cooked in the searing tandoor and knowing when to take them out was an art in itself.

The bright red-orange colour of meats cooked in the tandoor traditionally comes from a natural but flavourless dye called tandoori rang. This version of tandoori chicken gets its rich russet colour from saffron and a few drops of cochineal.

1 size 18 (1.8 kg) chicken, split into halves
1 teaspoon salt
1 tablespoon grated fresh ginger
1½ cups natural yoghurt
1 tablespoon lemon juice
1 teaspoon paprika
90 g ghee or butter, melted
fresh coriander leaves, to garnish
lemon wedges for serving

TANDOORI MIX

2 teaspoons ground turmeric
1 teaspoon paprika
½ teaspoon ground chillies
1 teaspoon garam masala
½ teaspoon ground cardamom
a good pinch of saffron threads or
   powdered saffron
a few drops of cochineal (optional)

SERVES 4–5

Combine all ingredients for the tandoori mix and set aside. Skin the chicken and make slashes in the flesh for the marinade to penetrate. Combine the salt, ginger, tandoori mix, yoghurt, lemon juice and paprika in a wide glass or china dish. Add chicken and turn to coat thoroughly with the marinade. Cover and chill for at least 6 hours, preferably overnight.

Preheat the oven to 200°C (400°F). Line a baking dish with a double sheet of aluminium foil and arrange the chicken halves, breast-side up, on it. Drizzle with melted ghee or butter and roast for 20 minutes. Turn chicken pieces over and continue cooking for another 15 minutes. Turn them again and cook breast-side up for the last 10 minutes of cooking. Baste the chicken frequently during cooking with the melted ghee and fat from the pan. Cut into large joint-sized pieces.

Garnish the chicken with coriander leaves and serve with lemon wedges, onion rings and warmed naan bread.

TIP - One of the secrets of tandoori chicken is the yoghurt marinade — the longer the chicken is left in the marinade, the more authentic the finished dish will be.

Naan

2 cups plain flour
½ teaspoon baking powder
1 teaspoon salt
1 teaspoon sugar
1 teaspoon active dry yeast
⅔ cup milk
⅔ cup natural yoghurt
1 egg, beaten
2 teaspoons poppy seeds (optional)

MAKES 6-8

Sift the flour, baking powder, salt and sugar into a bowl. Mix the yeast to a paste with a little of the milk. Beat the yoghurt into the remaining milk and heat until lukewarm. Stir in the yeast paste. Add this mixture gradually to the flour and mix to a dough. Knead well then add the egg and knead again. Cover the dough with a damp cloth and leave in a warm place for 1½ hours or until double its size.

Preheat the oven to 230°C (450°F). Cut the dough into 6-8 pieces. Roll into balls and flatten with your hands. Dip your fingertips into the poppy seeds (if using) and press into the naan. Place on baking sheets and bake for 12 minutes or until the naan are puffed and blistered. Serve hot.

Devilled Grilled Chicken

'There's a little devil dancing in your laughing Irish eyes,' I'd sing as a child. 'Margaret, we won't have any talk of the devil in this house!' My mother's rebuke brought an abrupt end to my cheerful singing. I had offended her by singing about the devil, but the word was to become very popular when I was growing up — as a way of enticing those who loved spicy foods.

Now that South-East Asian food is eaten so often and we are learning what 'hot' really means, 'devilled' dishes like this one probably seem mild. I've been making this dish since the 1960s, and it's a great way to add flavour to everyday chicken. Spatchcock are best eaten with fingers, as they are rather fiddly and bony.

4 small spatchcock or 8 chicken marylands
2 teaspoons salt
2 teaspoons sugar
1 teaspoon dry mustard
1 teaspoon ground ginger
freshly ground black pepper
1 teaspoon mild curry powder
60 g butter, melted
2 tablespoons tomato chutney or ketchup
1 tablespoon Worcestershire sauce
1 tablespoon light soy sauce
1 tablespoon fruit chutney
a dash of Tabasco sauce
lime wedges for serving

SERVES 4–6

Dry chicken pieces well with paper towels and remove any excess fat. Cut the drumsticks from the thighs to speed cooking. If using spatchcock, split down the back using poultry scissors and remove most of the backbone. Clean and dry well with a paper towel. Mix the salt, sugar and spices together and rub well into the surface of the chicken. Leave to marinate for at least 1 hour.

Arrange the chicken on a foil-lined grill rack and brush with a little of the butter. Place under a hot grill for 10 minutes, turning once after 6 minutes. Keep a careful eye on the chicken to watch for burning and cover with foil when necessary.

Meanwhile, add the remaining ingredients to the leftover butter and spoon over the chicken. Continue to grill, basting with the mixture for a further 10 minutes or until the juices run clear when a thigh or thick part is pricked with a skewer. Serve with salad greens and lime wedges.

NOTE ~ Grilling is a good method of cooking the smallest and youngest chickens, though they do need butter to keep them moist, as well as some additions for flavour.

Thai Red Duck Curry

I can't resist buying a barbecued duck whenever I go to Chinatown. The Chinese are experts at cooking it. Thai red duck curry, or Kaeng Phed Ped Yang, is traditionally served in Thailand at family celebrations such as weddings and the New Year. This is a tasty, simple recipe and a fabulous way of using ready-made Thai curry paste.

1 Chinese barbecued duck
1 tablespoon red curry paste
1⅓ cups coconut milk
½ cup water or Chicken Stock (page 237)
1 x 560 g can rambutan or lychees, drained
1 cup chopped fresh pineapple
1 cup fresh or frozen peas
2 tablespoons fish sauce
4 fresh kaffir lime leaves, very thinly sliced
10 cherry tomatoes
Thai basil leaves, to garnish

SERVES 4

Use a sharp knife to cut large portions of duck flesh off the carcass, leaving skin on. Cut into 2 cm slices and set aside.

Heat a wok or large saucepan on high. Add curry paste and half of the coconut milk. Cook, stirring, for 2–3 minutes. Add the remaining coconut milk, water or stock, rambutan or lychees, pineapple, peas, fish sauce and lime leaves. Bring to the boil, then reduce heat and simmer gently for 3 minutes. Add duck slices and tomatoes and simmer for another 5 minutes. Garnish with Thai basil leaves and serve with steamed rice.

COOKING THE DUCK YOURSELF

Split the duck in half using poultry scissors and a strong knife, removing all the noticeable fat. Season and place skin-side up on a rack in a pan. Roast in a preheated 200°C (400°F) oven for 10 minutes to render some of the fat from under the skin, then let the duck cool. Pour off rendered fat. Reduce oven to 180°C (350°F) and continue cooking for about 30 minutes, until tender, or done to taste. When cool, remove bones and cut into 2 cm slices as above.

Stuffed Roast Pork

While making a television appearance in England, I exchanged recipes with Clement Freud, a relative of the famous Sigmund Freud. Clement was a colourful force to be reckoned with in England during the 1970s, often mixing food with television and debating talents.

Pork belly stuffed and roasted in this way has all the flavour of a more expensive cut and, best of all, it has lots of crunchy crackling. I have varied it over time, sometimes using chopped spinach and a good butcher's pork sausage instead of mince, and dried apricots instead of prunes.

Creamy mashed or oven-roasted potatoes are a suitable accompaniment, or even just crusty bread. It's also very good cold, sliced and served with salad.

1 x 1.25 kg boned pork belly

STUFFING
2 onions, finely diced
4 cloves garlic, finely chopped
30 g butter
2 cups fresh breadcrumbs
½ cup milk
8 prunes, pitted and chopped
500 g minced pork
2 teaspoons each chopped thyme,
    sage and rosemary
salt and freshly ground black pepper
¼ teaspoon grated nutmeg
grated rind of ½ lemon

SERVES 6-8

Ask your butcher to bone the pork belly and score the rind. With a sharp knife, cut a slit right through the centre of the meat to form a pocket for the stuffing. This is easier if you start cutting from the short ends, meeting in the middle, and leaving the long sides intact to hold the stuffing.

To make the stuffing, cook the onions and garlic in the butter until softened, for about 5 minutes. Meanwhile, soak breadcrumbs in the milk until absorbed. In a large bowl combine breadcrumbs, prunes, minced pork, onions and garlic, seasonings and lemon. The stuffing needs only light handling; don't compact it. Spoon the stuffing into the pocket in the pork.

Preheat the oven to 230°C (445°F). Lightly grease a baking dish large enough to hold the pork lying flat and place the meat in it, skin-side up. Rub skin with a little salt and bake for 25–30 minutes, until the skin has blistered. Reduce heat to 190°C (375°F) and continue cooking for a further 45 minutes.

Remove the meat and place on a hot serving platter. Leave to rest for at least 5 minutes and then cut across into slices, taking a piece of crackling with each serving. Serve with gravy and creamy mashed potatoes (page 106). >>

Gravy

To make the gravy, pour off all but 1½ tablespoons of fat from the pan, add 2 tablespoons of plain flour and stir over a medium heat until browned. Pour in 2 cups of stock and stir until thick and smooth. Season with salt and freshly ground pepper and pour into a gravy boat.

Creamy mashed potatoes

Peel 6 medium potatoes and put into a saucepan of cold, lightly salted water to cover. Cook with the lid on the pan for about 15 minutes until the potatoes are easily pierced with a fork. Drain thoroughly, then shake the pan over the heat for a minute, until all surplus moisture has evaporated and the potatoes are quite dry. Mash with a potato masher or put through a potato ricer. Beat the potatoes with a wooden spoon until very smooth. Scald ½–1 cup of milk. Add 30 g of butter to the potatoes, then gradually beat in the hot milk until the potatoes are light and fluffy. Season with salt and freshly ground pepper.

To keep potatoes hot without spoiling

Cook the potatoes as described above, then mash and press down well in a saucepan with a potato masher. Pack tightly, levelling the top. Add 30 g of butter, spoon about 4 tablespoons of hot milk over, cover with a tight-fitting lid and leave in a warm place. Before serving, beat well, adding more hot milk if necessary. The potatoes will keep this way for up to 20 minutes.

Shoulder of Lamb with Two Heads of Garlic

The secret to this recipe is the long, slow cooking on the bone together with the foil cover, and every time I make it I'm asked how it's done. Cooking a shoulder of lamb for 3 hours makes the meat so tender that it almost pulls away from the bone in large pieces for serving, and the lamb juices give a delicious flavour to the potatoes baking underneath. The anchovies, garlic and vinegar work wonders, too. For a crowd, you can cook two shoulders in a bigger baking dish and increase the other ingredients. Cooking time will be the same.

1.5–2 kg lamb shoulder, trimmed of excess fat
salt and freshly ground black pepper
1 kg potatoes, peeled and thinly sliced
2 medium onions, thinly sliced
4 anchovy fillets
1 tablespoon olive oil
30 g butter
2–3 whole heads of garlic
sprig of fresh rosemary, broken into pieces
1½ tablespoons white wine vinegar
2 cups water

SERVES 4–6

Preheat the oven to 180°C (350°F). Rub lamb with salt and pepper. Heat a heavy baking dish on a moderate-high heat. Add lamb and brown all over. Lift out of the pan and place on a plate.

Spread potato and onion slices in layers in the baking dish, topping with anchovy fillets, olive oil and butter, and seasoning with salt and pepper. Remove any excess papery skin from garlic and cut widthwise in halves. Push garlic among the potatoes and onions. Lay lamb on top, sprinkle with rosemary and vinegar and pour over the water.

Cover tightly with foil and bake for 3 hours, removing foil halfway through cooking and reducing heat to 160°C (320°F).

To serve, transfer lamb to a hot platter with the vegetables. Cut meat off in chunky pieces and give each person half a head of garlic from which they can scoop out the tender flesh to season the lamb. Serve with a green salad.

TIP ~ If you'll be away from the kitchen for some time, cook lamb initially for 2½ hours at 160°C (320°F), remove foil, then increase heat to 190°C (375°F) to brown the edges of the potatoes and meat.

Thai Pork Roast with Garlic

Trader Vic's was an exotic Tahitian-style restaurant chain that I visited in New York and Honolulu in the 1960s. The food was out of this world: a typical dish was roast pork with cumin and wonderfully sweet fresh pineapple.

This is a lovely festive party dish when served alongside other dishes with Asian flavours. The rind is removed in this recipe, but can be baked separately in a hot oven if you want crackling (see page 112). I try to get banana leaves and fern fronds to decorate the table when I make this dish — even though it is Thai, for me it is so reminiscent of those days and Trader Vic's.

2 teaspoons ground cumin
6 cloves garlic, crushed with a little
    sea salt
plenty of freshly ground black pepper
1 x 2 kg pork loin, neck or boned and rolled
    shoulder, rind removed
1 fresh pineapple
4 tablespoons light soy sauce
¼ cup rice or white wine vinegar
6 tablespoons brown sugar
6 tablespoons chopped fresh coriander leaves

SERVES 8–10

Preheat the oven to 180°C (350°F). Combine the cumin, garlic and pepper and rub well into the meat.

Cut the skin from the pineapple and use some of it to cover the piece of pork. Place the pork on a rack in a baking dish and bake for about 1¼ hours or until almost tender.

Discard the pineapple skin, then baste the meat with a mixture of the soy sauce, vinegar and sugar, with half the chopped coriander. Return to the oven for a further 15 minutes, basting frequently. Remove the pork from the oven and place on a platter, skim the fat from the sauce and serve the sauce with the meat. Cut the pineapple into spears or rings and use to garnish the pork along with the remaining coriander. Serve warm or at room temperature, carved into slices, with plain steamed rice.

Baked Guinness Ham

Ever since I was a child, the youngest of six in a very social, busy family, I have relished the air of excitement when preparing for a party. I have never outgrown this and, no matter how small the occasion, I still get a lot of pleasure from planning a menu. At Christmas I prepare a glazed ham, baked with the flavours of Guinness stout, sugar and spice, and the outside caramelised so that each slice has a perfect mix of flavours.

Once during a radio interview I was asked for my recipe for baking a ham with Guinness stout. The switchboard was soon swamped with callers, claiming it as 'the best' and telling me how their families threaten not to come home for Christmas unless their mum cooks Margaret Fulton's baked Guinness ham!

1 x 5–6 kg cooked ham
2 cans or 1 large bottle Guinness stout
whole cloves (optional)
sprigs of watercress or flat-leaf parsley,
    to garnish

GLAZE
1 cup sugar
2 teaspoons dry mustard
2 teaspoons ground cardamom
2 teaspoons ground ginger
extra 2–3 tablespoons stout

SERVES UP TO 22

Preheat the oven to 160°C (320°F). Cut the skin of the ham around the thick end of the knuckle (it can be made into a scallop pattern) without cutting into the fat and flesh. Ease the skin from the fat by slipping your thumb under the skin, and firmly sliding it back and forth. Turn the ham over and ease away the rest of the skin, which should come off in one piece. Place the ham, fat-side up, in a roasting pan with the stout, reserving 2–3 tablespoons of stout for the glaze. Cover tightly with foil and bake for 1½ hours. Lift the foil and baste the ham with the drippings several times during the cooking.

Remove from the oven, take off the foil and pour off the liquid in the pan. Using a sharp knife, score fat with diagonal cuts at 4 cm intervals, first one way, then the opposite way, to form a diamond pattern.

For the glaze, mix the sugar, mustard and spices together with the reserved stout (enough to make a thick paste).

Spread half the glaze mixture over the ham and stud a clove in the corner of each diamond if you like. Increase the oven temperature to 200°C (400°F), and bake for another 30–40 minutes, basting every 10 minutes with remaining glaze. If serving hot, leave the ham in the turned-off oven for 30 minutes. If serving cold, cool and store in refrigerator overnight. Serve in thin slices. Place ham slices on a large serving platter and garnish with watercress or parsley.

CARVING THE HAM

Use a very sharp knife, preferably with a long, thin blade. The easiest way to carve a ham is to cut a wedge out first, about two thirds along the leg, and carve slices each side. This allows for a good distribution of lean and fat in each slice, as well as making manageable slices. Cold ham is cut in thin slices, but a hot ham may be cut into thicker slices. Before carving, wrap a sheet of foil around the knuckle. The carver can cover this with a clean napkin, and hold the ham without getting greasy.

STORING THE HAM

Cover with a clean tea towel or light cheesecloth bag that has been dipped in a solution of about 2 cups of water with 1 tablespoon of vinegar, and then squeezed out. Replace the tea towel every three days with another one to keep the ham moist and fresh.

Country-style Roast Pork

Can't get the crackling light and crisp? This was the problem faced by a chef at a pub in Berrima, New South Wales, one day when I dropped in after having spent the morning in the country. I expressed disappointment when no crackling arrived with my order of roast pork, and was told that the skin hadn't crisped enough and was unsuitable to serve. So I asked, 'Could the chef pop some under the grill for me?' Within minutes the waitress returned with lovely crisp crackling. If all else fails place the skin under the grill while the meat is 'resting', taking care not to let it catch. It will soon 'bubble' and become crisp.

Here's how to make a roast pork dinner with the all-important crispy crackling, sauce, gravy and baked plums. Whereas once it was important to cook the pork thoroughly, today it can be served medium-rare with a little pink juice for ultimate moistness. Suit yourself, however, and cook it the way your family prefers, allowing 20–30 minutes cooking time per 500 g, plus 30 minutes extra.

1 x 1.5–2 kg pork loin (boned or left on the bone with the chops chined), leg or shoulder
6 sage leaves
1 tablespoon olive oil
sea salt
6 potatoes, peeled and halved

SERVES 8

Ask your butcher to score the skin of the pork in narrow strips or a diamond pattern. Preheat the oven to 230°C (445°F). Weigh the pork and ascertain the cooking time (see above). Pierce the flesh in several different places with a sharp pointed knife and insert the sage leaves. Place on a roasting rack in a baking tray and rub the skin all over with oil then sea salt.

Roast for 30 minutes or until the skin is crisp and golden. Meanwhile, drop the potatoes into a saucepan of boiling salted water and cook for 5 minutes. Drain and score lightly with a fork.

Reduce heat to 180°C (350°F), add the potatoes to the tray and roast for 45–60 minutes, turning the potatoes several times. If the loin is on the bone use a sharp knife to remove the chine bone and loosen the meat. To make carving easier, remove the crackling in sections. Carve the meat across into thick slices.

Serve hot with seasonal green vegetables. Also delicious with roast pork are apple sauce, rhubarb and orange sauce, gravy or baked plums (see overleaf). >>

Apple sauce

Make apple sauce by peeling, coring and quartering 3 golden delicious or granny smith apples. Place in a small saucepan with ½ cup of water, 1 tablespoon of sugar and 1 strip of lemon rind. Cover and cook gently to a pulp. Rub through a coarse sieve, rinse out the saucepan and return the apple purée to it. Cook fairly rapidly, stirring continuously until the purée will just drop from the spoon. Serve hot.

Rhubarb and orange sauce

Wash and cut a bundle of rhubarb into 5 cm lengths. Place in a heavy-based saucepan with a nut of butter, the grated rind and juice from an orange and 1 tablespoon of brown sugar. Cover and cook on a low heat for 8–10 minutes. Leave until cool.

Gravy

To make gravy, skim off all but 1 tablespoon of the fat in the baking tray. Sprinkle over 1½ tablespoons of plain flour and cook, stirring continuously until browned. Stir in 3 cups of chicken or vegetable stock and cook, scraping any bits from the bottom and sides of the pan, until gravy thickens slightly. Simmer for 1 minute. Season to taste with salt and freshly ground black pepper.

Baked plums

Wash 750 g of plums and remove stones. Make a shallow cut in each plum and place in a separate baking tray. Place ½ cup of liquid from the meat baking tray, ¼ cup of red wine and 55 g of sugar in a jug and stir until the sugar is dissolved. Pour over the plums, cover with foil and bake until tender while the pork is cooking, for about 15 minutes.

Crusted Racks of Lamb

When I was a girl, lamb was a regular dish at our table — and very little of it was wasted. My mother knew how to cook brains the French way with black butter sauce, and she cooked lambs fry as carefully as a good Italian restaurant does veal liver, sliced thinly and flashed in the pan. The neck went into a delicious stew with parsley, potatoes and lemon juice to give it punch and, of course, a good Scotch broth was never far away. The leg and shoulder were often the roast, with the rack of lamb usually turned into cutlets that we crumbed and fried.

These days I love to roast a rack of lamb — it's hard to spoil and easy to carve. I give it a crunchy herb and breadcrumb crust, which helps to protect the lamb during cooking and makes it particularly tender.

30 g butter, melted
¼ cup chopped flat-leaf parsley
1 teaspoon chopped thyme
½ teaspoon salt
freshly ground black pepper
rind and juice of 1 lemon
1½ cups fresh breadcrumbs
2 Frenched racks of lamb (6 cutlets to a rack)
1–2 tablespoons Dijon mustard

SERVES 4

Preheat the oven to 220°C (430°F). Mix the butter with the parsley, thyme, salt, pepper, lemon rind and juice, and breadcrumbs. Heat a baking tray over a high heat and sear the lamb racks for a few minutes, meat-side down, until browned. Cool slightly then spread the meat side of the rack thickly with Dijon mustard. Press breadcrumb mixture onto the mustard in a thick layer.

Place lamb on a roasting rack in the baking tray and roast for 10–15 minutes. When lamb is cooked the juices will run clear. Remove from the oven, cover loosely with foil and leave to rest for 5–10 minutes. Cut racks into halves to make 4 pieces, or cut the cutlets from the racks carefully so as not to disturb the crumb crust.

TIP - For convenience, the lamb can be topped with crumbs ahead of time, ready for roasting.

Butterflied Leg of Lamb, Bengal Style

The 1950s and 1960s were memorable times for dinner parties and entertaining. Our dear friend Jean Storey, who later wrote under the name Jane Tennant, was one of the first to make a good French terrine in this country, and her husband Peter was one of the first to barbecue a butterflied leg of lamb.

The leg of lamb is boned and opened out like a butterfly (a butcher can do this for you), so that it can be barbecued flat on the grill. I like to cook it in what I call a 'Bengal style' by rubbing it first with spices and yoghurt so that the flavours permeate the meat. It takes less than an hour to cook to a rich brown outside with the thin portions well done and the thick portions slightly pink.

1 x 2 kg butterflied leg of lamb
juice of 1 lemon
1 teaspoon ground cardamom
2 teaspoons ground coriander
½ teaspoon ground turmeric
½ cup natural yoghurt
salt and freshly ground black pepper

SERVES 6–8

With a sharp knife make 5 mm incisions into any thick portions of the leg of lamb. Rub the lemon juice and combined spices into the lamb, then spread the yoghurt over the surface and leave to marinate in a glass dish for 1–2 hours.

Remove the meat from the marinade. Using a sharp knife, score the skin with diagonal cuts at 4 cm intervals, first one way, then the opposite way, to form a diamond pattern. Place it skin-side down on a greased grill 10 cm above glowing coals (see Tip). Baste frequently with the marinade and turn occasionally. Cook for about 1 hour.

To carve, start at one end, and thinly slice across the grain. Season with salt and pepper to taste.

TIP - If you don't have a barbecue you can roast the lamb in a hot oven at 220°C (430°F) for about 40 minutes, turning once or twice during cooking.

Roasted Racks of Lamb with Baby Vegetables

This dish takes a new look at meat and three vegetables. The vegetables can be varied depending on what you have to hand. If you don't have baby vegetables, longer ones can be cut into lengths. If you like potatoes, they can be quartered, put in the steamer first and given an eight-minute start. Vary the vegetables to fit in with the seasons. The mint pesto is a wonderful garnish, but the dish is just as flavoursome without it.

2 Frenched racks of lamb (6 cutlets to a rack)
1 tablespoon mixed chopped herbs such as
    flat-leaf parsley, oregano or thyme
salt and freshly ground black pepper
1 tablespoon olive oil
200 g baby carrots, halved lengthwise
200 g baby zucchini, halved lengthwise
200 g baby beans
150 g baby spinach leaves
30 g butter
1 quantity Mint Pesto (page 234)

SERVES 4

Preheat the oven to 220°C (430°F). Season the lamb with herbs, salt and pepper. Arrange on a roasting rack in a deep baking tray, drizzle with oil and roast for 10–15 minutes or until juices run clear. Rest the tray for 5–10 minutes in a warm place, covered loosely with foil.

Prepare a steamer with boiling water and steam all vegetables except spinach leaves, half-covered with the lid for 3–5 minutes, until just tender. Before serving, heat the butter in a frying pan and toss vegetables with the spinach leaves to heat and coat with butter. Season to taste.

To serve, spoon vegetables onto each plate, cut the lamb racks into halves to make 4 pieces, or divide into cutlets, and arrange on top. Drizzle mint pesto over each serving. Spoon over juices from the baking dish.

NOTE - Steamers are inexpensive — department stores have expandable ones that fit any saucepan.

Beef Stroganoff

What happens when food is prepared on a prime-time TV show? I once cooked beef stroganoff and the presenter took a mouthful and was amazed that something so easy to cook could taste so good. Then the cameraman and the soundman sampled the stroganoff. After the show they all boasted they would make the dish that night.

Beef stroganoff was created for Count Stroganov of imperial Russia as an after-theatre supper dish. It later became popular in restaurants in China before the start of the Second World War. Chinese and Russian immigrants then introduced the dish to the United States where it was popular with the fine dining crowd during the 1950s. It was traditionally served with crisp straw potatoes, but is now more often served with noodles or rice, which suggests a Chinese influence.

750 g fillet steak, cut into pencil-thin slices, then into strips
salt and freshly ground black pepper
1 tablespoon plain flour
60 g butter
2 medium onions, finely sliced
200–250 g button mushrooms, finely sliced
1 tablespoon tomato paste
2/3 cup sour cream

SERVES 4

Season the beef strips well with salt and pepper and toss in the flour. Melt half the butter in a frying pan, add the onions and fry slowly, stirring, for about 10 minutes, until just coloured. Add the mushrooms and fry for a few minutes, adding more butter if necessary.

Remove the onions and mushrooms, add the remaining butter to the pan and when hot add the beef strips and fry briskly for 3–4 minutes.

Return the onions and mushrooms to the pan with plenty of salt and pepper. Shake over the heat for 1 minute, add the tomato paste and sour cream, then cook for a few minutes longer until heated through. Serve immediately or keep warm by standing the pan in hot water for 15–20 minutes only. Serve with boiled rice, noodles or with triangles of hot buttered toast.

NOTE ~ Don't make this one ahead; it's a last-minute dish and takes only minutes to cook. And best not to attempt this rec ipe for a crowd — a large quantity of beef tends to stew and the dish loses its fresh quality.

Saltimbocca

Veal steaks, also known as scaloppini or escalopes, are very quick to cook. Ask your butcher to cut the veal steaks thinly rather than bat them out, which causes them to shrink more during cooking.

Saltimbocca tastes so good and is so quick to prepare that it 'jumps in the mouth', as the Italian name states. There are many versions of this Roman dish, some of which include cheese. This is one of the simplest and, according to my research, most authentic versions of this recipe.

8 fresh sage leaves
4 thin veal steaks, halved
4 slices prosciutto, halved
45 g butter
¾ cup dry white wine
salt and freshly ground black pepper
a little extra butter (optional)

SERVES 4

Place a sage leaf on each slice of meat, top with prosciutto and secure with toothpicks. Melt the butter in a frying pan, add meat slices in several batches and brown quickly on both sides, turning carefully so as not to disturb the prosciutto and sage leaf. Remove and keep warm while frying remaining pieces.

Arrange the veal on a serving dish and keep warm. Add the wine to pan with a little salt and plenty of pepper. Stir and scrape the base well to incorporate the tasty bits stuck to the bottom of the pan. A small nut of butter can be swirled in for a richer sauce. Spoon the sauce over the veal and serve with steamed potatoes and a green vegetable or tossed salad.

Veal steaks with a mustard cream sauce

Dust the veal steaks first with a little seasoned flour, shaking off excess. Fry quickly, then keep warm. Add ½ cup of white wine to the pan with a tablespoon of Dijon mustard and ½ cup of pouring cream. Stir and simmer for 2 minutes or so. Serve the veal with sauce spooned over. This is good with buttered noodles or rice and a salad.

Malayan Beef Satays

This recipe appeared in my first cookbook and, following the book's launch, was one that I chose to demonstrate — often at large shopping centres — when I was travelling around Australia and England.

No chilli is used, rather good-quality, freshly ground cumin makes the difference. Make sure that some fat is included with the meat or the satays will be dry. Cooking satays on a charcoal barbecue achieves that authentic flavour; however, you can get a satisfactory result with a red-hot grill.

1 kg sirloin steak, cut into 2 cm cubes
⅓ cup light soy sauce
⅓ cup peanut oil
2 onions, finely diced
2 cloves garlic, crushed
2 teaspoons ground cumin
3 tablespoons toasted sesame seeds
1 teaspoon lemon juice
salt and freshly ground black pepper

SATAY SAUCE
2 onions, chopped
1 tablespoon water
1 tablespoon chilli powder
2 tablespoons vegetable oil
¾ cup coconut milk
juice of 1 lemon
1 tablespoon brown sugar
⅔ cup crunchy peanut butter
salt
wedges of lemon or lime for serving

SERVES 6

Place the meat in a bowl and add the soy sauce, peanut oil, onions, garlic, cumin, sesame seeds and lemon juice. Turn to coat the meat thoroughly and leave to marinate for 3 hours. Meanwhile, soak bamboo skewers in enough water to cover, to prevent them from burning when cooking. Drain the meat, reserving the marinade. Thread the steak cubes onto the skewers.

Grill the skewers over hot coals or under the grill for 6–8 minutes, basting with marinade and turning frequently. Season with salt and pepper. To make the satay sauce, blend the onions and water in a food processor until finely chopped. Transfer to a small bowl and stir in the chilli powder.

Heat the oil in a medium-sized saucepan over a medium heat. Add the onion mixture and cook for 5 minutes, stirring, until aromatic and the onion is soft. Add the coconut milk, lemon juice and sugar and simmer for 5 minutes. Add the peanut butter, mix well and simmer for another 5 minutes, until sauce has thickened slightly.

Season with salt to taste. Serve skewers with satay sauce, steamed rice, wedges of lemon or lime and chunks of cucumber.

Beef Strips in Tomato Cream Sauce

Anyone who has gone on a group holiday will be familiar with the custom of sharing the cooking of the evening meals. On one holiday, I took several frozen containers of this dish and a few tubs of sour cream. It's great for a big group or party and is known among my friends and those who bought my early cookbooks as 'stroganoff for a crowd', as it is indeed made with beef strips, onions and tomatoes and finished with sour cream. Make it one or two days before your gathering and store in the refrigerator, adding the sour cream when almost ready to serve after reheating.

2 kg round or chuck steak, cut into
   thin strips
½ cup plain flour, seasoned with salt
   and freshly ground black pepper
60 g butter
2 tablespoons oil
2 large onions, finely diced
4 cloves garlic, crushed
2 cups diced green capsicum
500 g button mushrooms, sliced and sautéed
   in a little oil and butter
2 x 400 g cans chopped tomatoes
1 cup water
2 tablespoons Worcestershire sauce
3 cups sour cream

SERVES 10–12

Coat the beef strips with seasoned flour. Heat half the butter and 1 tablespoon of the oil in a frying pan and sauté the meat in 3 or 4 batches until brown. Add the remaining butter and oil when required. Place in a large saucepan.

Add the onions, garlic and capsicum to the frying pan over a medium heat and cook for 5 minutes, stirring, until softened. Add to the beef with the mushrooms, tomatoes, water and Worcestershire sauce. Bring slowly to the boil, then reduce the heat and simmer gently for 1 hour.

Remove from the heat and stir in the sour cream. Replace over low heat, stirring until mixture is hot, without letting it boil. Taste and check for seasoning. Serve with parsley rice.

Parsley Rice

3 cups long-grain rice
1 teaspoon salt
60 g butter
½ cup chopped flat-leaf parsley

SERVES 10–12

Fill 2 large heavy-based saucepans each with 4–5 cups of water and bring to the boil. Sprinkle half the rice and half the salt into each saucepan. Cover tightly and simmer gently for 20 minutes, until all liquid is absorbed. Fluff up the rice with a fork, adding butter and parsley to each, and serve hot.

Steak au Poivre

At a very young age I learnt that the most important thing when cooking was to have good ingredients, and that means shopping carefully. As a girl, if I went to the butcher and bought a piece of steak that was thick one end and thin the other I would be sent back to the shop with it. My mother would say, 'Watch what you're buying, Margaret. It's good money that's going into it. How can I cook this? It's got to be the same thickness right through.'

Peppercorns are sold in different grades, but only freshly cracked black peppercorns will release the peppery oil that flavours the steak so perfectly in this classic dish. Crack the pepper with a mortar and pestle, or with a mallet between two sheets of plastic.

4 steaks (185–250 g), rump, porterhouse
　　or fillet
2–3 tablespoons coarsely cracked
　　black peppercorns
2 tablespoons brandy (optional)
a dash of Tabasco sauce (optional)
a dash of Worcestershire sauce
a little lemon juice
60 g butter
sea salt
2 tablespoons chopped flat-leaf parsley
　　or chives
2 tablespoons cream (optional)

SERVES 4

Sprinkle both sides of each steak with pepper and press well into the meat with the heel of your hand. Let stand at room temperature for 30 minutes.

Heat a lightly oiled, large heavy-based frying pan over a high heat, add the steaks and cook on one side until brown, for about 3 minutes. Turn steaks and cook for another 3–4 minutes, until brown on the other side and cooked to taste. Remove from the pan and leave to rest for 5 minutes in a warm place, loosely covered with foil.

Return the pan to a medium heat and add the brandy, if using, scraping up the browned bits on the bottom of the pan with a wooden spoon for 30 seconds. Add sauces and lemon juice to taste, then whisk in the butter until completely melted. Taste and adjust the seasonings, adding a little salt, and sprinkle with parsley or chives. For a creamy sauce, swirl cream into the pan sauce. Spoon the sauce over the steaks and serve.

Steak au poivre vert

Prepare as for steak au poivre (above) but replace the black peppercorns with poivre vert, the soft green peppercorns that are sold pickled in brine.

Steak Diane

During the 1950s and 1960s, dishes that could be prepared at the restaurant table and flamed with showman flair were popular in top eateries. The maître d' would stand beside a gueridon — a tableside cart — with a small burner on it and in front of us produce dazzling spectacles such as steak Diane. I prefer to make this dish for two people only, because then I know I can have the steaks cooked perfectly. My routine is to first put on the potatoes for Creamy Mashed Potatoes (page 106) and, while they're cooking, prepare the steak and ingredients for the sauce, and then make a salad and set the table. The steak takes one and a half minutes, so everything should be ready before you start cooking it. Oh, and before that, make sure someone has uncorked the red wine to let it breathe!

FOR EACH PERSON YOU WILL NEED:
1 thick slice (about 4 cm) fillet steak
salt and freshly ground black pepper
30 g butter
2 tablespoons finely chopped flat-leaf parsley
1 clove garlic, finely chopped
1 tablespoon snipped chives (optional)
about 1 tablespoon Worcestershire sauce
1 tablespoon brandy

Trim any fat and gristle from the steak, then slice almost through the centre and open out, butterfly-fashion. Place the steak between 2 pieces of plastic wrap and flatten with a rolling pin to no thicker than 6 mm. Season lightly with salt and pepper.

Heat half the butter in a heavy-based frying pan and, when sizzling, add the steak. Shake the pan to stop the meat from sticking, then start timing: cook for 40 seconds on the first side for rare, 1 minute for medium. Have the heat high enough for the steak to brown quickly and, if necessary, add the remaining butter.

Turn the steak over and sprinkle with half the parsley and garlic. Cook until done to your liking and sprinkle with the remaining parsley and garlic, adding chives if using, and Worcestershire sauce. Heat the brandy in a small pan, set alight and pour over the steak. Shake the frying pan to distribute the sauce, turning the steak over in it, then transfer to a warm plate and pour the pan juices over.

Daube of Beef Provençale

This dish has been in my family for generations; in fact, since my sister Jean lived in France in the 1940s. She taught it to Suzanne, who included it in her first book on French cooking in the early 1970s, and we have been making it ever since, always remembering Jean's words, 'Don't forget the orange rind.'

In those days beef cheek was hard to come by, but it's perfect for making a dish like this and is becoming more and more available. Just keep pestering your butcher if you can't get it and he'll eventually oblige. Otherwise use chuck, gravy or shin, or even blade steak, which has a good flavour and becomes beautifully tender with the long cooking. This dish can be made the day before and chilled, which allows the fat to set on the top and be lifted away before reheating.

1 kg lean beef, cut into large cubes
2 cloves garlic, finely chopped
3 tablespoons olive oil
1½ cups red wine
bouquet garni (page 15)
125 g thick slices pancetta, cubed (optional)
1 large onion, finely diced
2 carrots, thickly sliced
2 tomatoes, peeled and quartered
½ cup beef stock
1–2 strips orange rind
salt and freshly ground black pepper
freshly chopped flat-leaf parsley, to garnish

SERVES 6

Place the beef in a large glass bowl with the garlic, half the olive oil, the wine and the bouquet garni and marinate in a cool place for at least 3 hours. Heat the remaining oil in a flameproof casserole dish and sauté the pancetta (if using) for about 3 minutes until the fat is transparent.

Drain the beef, pouring the marinade into a saucepan. Boil rapidly until reduced by half. Meanwhile, add the beef to the pancetta and cook over a brisk heat until coloured. Add the onion and carrots to the casserole dish and cook for a further 5 minutes. When the marinade has reduced, add to the casserole dish with the bouquet garni. Add the tomatoes, stock and orange rind and season with salt and pepper. Cover and simmer gently for 2–2½ hours or until the meat is very tender.

Spoon the meat into a deep serving dish. Remove the bouquet garni from the sauce and skim the excess fat. Pour the sauce over the meat and garnish with parsley. Serve with Creamy Mashed Potatoes (see page 106).

Standing Rib Roast

A roast of beef, rump or sirloin, on or off the bone, must be one of the best meals in the world. When I plan a roast beef dinner I go to my butcher with an open mind about what cut I will buy. He stocks organic meats and chicken that are humanely raised. It may cost more than meat purchased from the supermarket, but my preference is to eat the best and have it less often.

There are several prime cuts of beef that work well when roasted: a large whole rump that may weigh about 4 kg; or a smaller cut off the rump — ask for the point end — of about 2 kg. Another top cut is a standing rib roast or rolled rib, while a convenient cut is a boned rib roast, which makes for easy carving.

1 x 2 kg beef rump or 1.5 kg boneless sirloin
1 teaspoon freshly ground black pepper
2 cloves garlic, crushed with a little sea salt
   (optional)
2 tablespoons olive oil

SERVES 6–8

Bring beef to room temperature. Preheat the oven to 220°C (430°F). Mix the pepper and garlic with the olive oil and rub over the surface of the meat. Place the beef on a roasting rack in a heavy baking dish. Roast for 20 minutes and then reduce heat to 180°C (350°F).

For rare beef the whole rump roast will take about 1 hour, or a boneless sirloin about 45 minutes. Allow an additional 15 minutes for medium-rare. Remove the beef from the oven and transfer to a warm plate, cover loosely with foil and leave to rest for 15–20 minutes in a warm place. Serve with Crusty Roasted Potatoes and Parsnips (page 148) or steamed vegetables, and gravy. >>

If you want to make gravy

Pour off all but 2 tablespoons of fat from the baking dish. Over a moderate heat, deglaze the pan with ½ cup of white wine and 1 tablespoon of sherry vinegar, scraping the bits from the bottom of the pan. Add 2 cups of beef stock and any juices from the meat, and cook for a few minutes. Season with salt and freshly ground black pepper to taste. Strain into a small saucepan and just before serving swirl in 2 teaspoons of butter, which will soften and thicken the gravy. Pour into a gravy boat.

ROASTING BEEF

A hot oven sears the outside of the meat, and with controlled temperature and timing you should achieve the results you want. Always remove the meat from the refrigerator in time for it to reach room temperature before cooking. The times for roasting prime beef vary, depending on the method, as you have the choice of quick-roasting or slow-roasting.

For quick-roasting, the meat is seared on top of the stove and then put in a hot oven at 220°C (430°F) for 20 minutes. The heat is then lowered to 180°C (350°F) for the rest of the cooking time. If you love the outside of the meat crusty and brown, then this is the method you will prefer. Allow 15 minutes for each 500 g plus an additional 15 minutes for medium–rare beef. Allow 20 minutes per 500 g for well-done meat, with an additional 20 minutes.

For slow-roasting, the meat is cooked at 160°C (320°F) for the entire cooking time. This gives moister meat with less shrinkage, but it does not give a crisp outside. Allow 30 minutes per 500 g and an additional 30 minutes. This gives a medium-done result. A joint of beef should not be over-seasoned — it has enough flavour itself, along with its traditional accompaniments. After it is cooked it should stand for 15–20 minutes in a warm place before being carved.

Vegetables and Salads

ARTICHOKES

Discovering the joys of the delectable artichoke is one of my happiest memories. A member of the thistle family, several varieties of artichoke come into season in early summer. When it is young and tender, the long, slightly purple Italian artichoke is often halved and fried, or stewed in wine or stock. The fried leaves look like bronze petals. The larger, rounder artichoke is more common and suitable for boiling, to be eaten leaf by leaf with melted butter or a dipping sauce.

Artichokes are enormous fun, especially when shared with family and friends. To eat an artichoke, remove leaves one by one and pull each leaf between the teeth to scrape away the tender base.

Discard the rest of the leaf. In the centre of older artichokes you will find the fuzzy choke. Spoon this out, discard and enjoy the heart of the artichoke. Provide small bowls of warm water with a slice of lemon for each person, for cleaning fingers.

To plain-boil artichokes, lower into boiling, salted water with a slice of lemon and simmer for 15–20 minutes — the exact time will depend on the age and size. A good way to test is to pull off an outer leaf, which should come away easily if cooked.

To trim and prepare artichokes

Remove outer leaves and then cut one-third off the top of the artichoke with a sharp knife. Trim the stalk with scissors, leaving a 5 cm stalk. As each one is prepared, rub the surface with a lemon to prevent discolouration.

Braised Stuffed Artichokes

This is an Italian way to cook artichokes. You can also add two or three chopped anchovies to the stuffing to add a Mediterranean touch.

6–8 young globe artichokes
1 cup fresh breadcrumbs
½ cup grated parmesan cheese
3 tablespoons chopped fresh herbs
    such as flat-leaf parsley, oregano or mint
salt and freshly ground black pepper
3 tablespoons olive oil
1 onion, chopped
1 large tomato, peeled, seeded and diced

SERVES 6

Trim and prepare the artichokes (see page 136). Make a stuffing by combining the breadcrumbs, cheese, herbs, salt and pepper and 1 tablespoon of the olive oil. Open the leaves of the artichokes slightly and fill spaces with the stuffing, pushing it down well into the base of the leaves. Drizzle with a little oil.

Stand artichokes in an oiled casserole dish or heavy saucepan. Pour in a little water and the remaining olive oil, then add the onion and tomato. Cover and cook over a low heat for 30 minutes, basting from time to time with the juices. Arrange the cooked artichokes on a serving dish and spoon over the juices.

Artichokes Braised in Wine and Garlic

Artichokes cooked gently with oil, wine and garlic are an epicurean treat.

4 globe artichokes
3 tablespoons olive oil
2 cloves garlic, crushed with a little sea salt
½ cup white wine
freshly ground black pepper

SERVES 2–4

Trim and prepare the artichokes (see page 136). Heat the olive oil in a large frying pan over a medium heat. Add the garlic, wine and artichokes. Cook the first side of the artichokes for about 5–8 minutes and then turn to cook the other side, pressing down well and cooking for another 5–8 minutes until the artichokes are tender. Older artichokes may take longer. Serve seasoned with plenty of pepper.

French-Style Peas

As a young mother, I would usually give the job of shelling peas to Suzanne or make it something we could do together as we chatted. If we were busy, however, we would use frozen peas for convenience and because they are often sweeter.

I love to remind people of this recipe. The peas are slow-cooked the French way: on a bed of shredded lettuce, often with a little bacon and onion, until much of the peas' bright colour is lost. The method makes peas very special.

1 kg peas in the pod or 500 g frozen peas
60 g butter
125 g streaky bacon, rind removed,
    cut into strips (optional)
6 spring onions or eschallots, finely
    sliced (including green tops of the
    spring onions)
½ lettuce or 6–8 outer lettuce leaves
a few sprigs of mint
1 teaspoon sugar
salt and freshly ground black pepper
2 tablespoons water

SERVES 4–6

Shell the peas (if necessary). Melt the butter in a flameproof casserole dish and gently fry the bacon, if using, and spring onions until soft but not brown. Wash the lettuce and shred finely. Add to the pan and stir over a low heat until the lettuce is bright green and juicy.

Add the shelled or frozen peas to the pan with one or two sprigs of mint, sugar, and salt and pepper to taste. Add the water, cover the casserole tightly and cook over a gentle heat for 15–20 minutes, or until peas are tender. To serve, remove the sprigs of mint and serve from the casserole dish with the pan juices and lettuce.

Carrots Vichy

A classic method of cooking carrots rather than simply boiling them, and one that I usually use for family meals. Young baby carrots need only to be scraped lightly and, if they are tiny, cooked whole. Larger carrots are best sliced thickly, or halved or quartered lengthwise, then cut into batons. Everyone loves the syrupy glaze that is left at the end of cooking.

1 kg young carrots
1 cup water
60 g butter
salt
1–2 tablespoons honey or sugar
2 tablespoons chopped flat-leaf
   parsley (optional)
freshly ground black pepper

SERVES 4–6

Peel the carrots and cut them into slices or thick matchsticks, or if tiny, leave whole. Place in a pan with the water, butter, salt and honey or sugar. Cover the pan and cook gently for about 10 minutes until almost tender. Remove the lid from the pan and cook briskly until the liquid has completely evaporated, taking care not to burn. Shake the pan frequently so that the carrots are thoroughly glazed with the sugar and butter. Toss with the parsley, if using, and pepper and serve piping hot.

POTATOES

Potatoes are at the top of my food must-haves list. I love them, like most Scots do. In fact, I should say that I love them like most Scots, Irish, French and Russians do! They are traditionally the food of the poor, who have discovered some of the best ways to cook them. Potatoes are equally good in haute cuisine creations. A chef has at his or her command more than 50 ways to present *pommes de terre*.

Know your potatoes

At my greengrocer, I can choose from fifteen or more potato varieties, including:

~ Sebago. Round in shape and large with white skin and flesh. A good all-round potato, particularly suitable for baking.

~ Red pontiac. Red-skinned with moist, white flesh. Pontiacs cook and store well and are particularly good mashed.

~ Delaware. Oval in shape with white skin and a firm, waxy flesh. Best boiled and baked.

~ Desiree. Long and oval with pink skin and yellow flesh. Best fried, boiled and baked.

~ New potatoes or chats. Round or oval in shape with thick skin and a firm, waxy flesh. Best boiled, though they can be pan-fried or sautéed with the skin on.

~ Tasmanian pink-eye or pink lady. These have a slight pink tint to the skin and yellow flesh. Best steamed and boiled.

Choosing and storing potatoes

When buying potatoes, avoid any variety that has green flesh or skin. Potatoes should feel firm and have a faint earthy smell. Store potatoes in a cool, dark place. They keep particularly well if left unwashed with the earth still clinging to the skin. Buy new potatoes in small quantities as they do not keep well.

Potatoes Dauphinoise

The mountain province of Dauphiné in France produces excellent potatoes, which are used in gratins — this dish is also known as gratin dauphinoise. Cheese is not always used but I like the addition of gruyère cheese. I often serve this potato dish with roast lamb or beef. As a Scot, I also recommend that you try stovies.

1 kg potatoes, preferably yellow-fleshed,
    peeled and cut into wafer-thin slices
salt and freshly ground black pepper
a little grated nutmeg
1 cup grated gruyère cheese (optional)
1 clove garlic, crushed
2 cups milk (or milk and cream)
30 g butter, cut into pieces

SERVES 6

Preheat the oven to 190°C (375°F). Butter a shallow gratin dish. Arrange a layer of potato slices and sprinkle with salt, pepper and nutmeg. Repeat layers until all potatoes are used. If using cheese, strew over each layer.

Add the garlic to the milk in a saucepan and heat until just scalded. Pour over the potatoes, dot with butter and cover loosely with foil.

Bake for about 1½ hours, adding more milk if necessary. If the liquid has not been absorbed after this time, remove the foil. The potatoes should be browned on top and creamy moist within. Serve hot from the dish.

Potatoes boulangère

Potatoes boulangère are cooked as for dauphinoise, with 2 sliced onions in place of the cheese, and chicken or beef stock in place of the milk.

Stovies

This is the Scottish version of gratin potatoes. Layer sliced potatoes with sliced onions in a gratin dish. Add tiny bits of butter here and there and season with salt and black pepper. Cover with beef stock and cook as above. For bacon stovies use bacon fat in place of the butter.

Potato Wedges Roasted with Wine

The wine used in the following recipe imparts a nice acidic flavour (think how popular salt and vinegar chips are, though this is much better). Serve the potatoes hot and crisp, as soon as they come from the oven. The rosemary sprigs may be replaced with oregano or thyme.

1 kg large roasting potatoes, such as desiree
2 tablespoons olive oil
½ cup dry white wine
sea salt and freshly ground black pepper
sprigs of rosemary
30 g butter

SERVES 6

Preheat the oven to 200°C (400F). Scrub the potatoes, if necessary. Peel potatoes or leave unpeeled, depending on taste, then halve and cut into thick wedges. Use paper towels or a tea towel to pat the potatoes dry. Place in a large roasting tray. Drizzle the olive oil and wine over and season generously. Scatter the rosemary sprigs, toss well and dot the potatoes with the butter. Bake for about 1 hour and 15 minutes, turning potatoes frequently until they are golden and crunchy.

Crispy Potatoes with Roasted Capsicum

There is something irresistible about the smell of fried potatoes. This dish not only looks and tastes great, but has the added bonus of being good for you.

2 red capsicums
750 g small red potatoes, such as desiree
¼ cup olive oil
¼ cup black olives, pitted
leaves from a few sprigs of rosemary
sea salt and freshly ground black pepper

SERVES 4

Place the capsicums on an oiled baking tray and grill under a high heat until blistered and blackened, turning frequently. Cool in a paper bag then scrape off the blackened skin and rinse. Cut into thick strips and set aside. Peel the potatoes and cut lengthwise into quarters. Rinse and dry thoroughly with paper towels.

In a large heavy-based frying pan, heat the oil over a medium–high heat until hot. Add the potatoes in a single layer. Reduce the heat to medium and brown the potatoes thoroughly on one side before turning. Fry the potatoes for about 15 minutes, until they are golden brown and crisp on all sides, and tender when pierced with a fork.

Add the capsicum strips, olives and rosemary to the pan and cook for a few minutes until heated through. Transfer to a warm serving bowl and season to taste with salt and a good grinding of pepper.

Crusty Garlic and Rosemary Potatoes

The following is a very Italian way to cook potatoes. The garlic and rosemary add a wonderfully fragrant dimension to the potatoes.

500 g small red or new potatoes, quartered
3 cloves garlic, sliced
1 tablespoon olive oil
1 teaspoon rosemary leaves
salt and freshly ground black pepper

SERVES 2–4

Steam the potatoes in a covered saucepan for 8 minutes or until just tender. In a heavy-based frying pan, cook the garlic in the oil over a medium heat, stirring, until pale golden. Add the potatoes, rosemary, salt and pepper.

Fry the potatoes over a medium–high heat, shaking the pan, for 5 minutes or until the potatoes are golden and fragrant with garlic and rosemary.

Crusty Roasted Potatoes and Parsnips

Potatoes and parsnips roasted this way have a wonderful crisp golden crust. You can add cloves of garlic to give the vegetables extra punch.

1 kg even-sized, medium potatoes such
    as desiree or pontiac, peeled and halved
    or quartered
¼ cup olive oil
sprigs of rosemary (optional)
sea salt and freshly ground black pepper
3 parsnips, scraped lightly and halved
4–6 cloves garlic (optional)

SERVES 6

Preheat the oven to 200°C (400°F). Place the potatoes in a medium-sized saucepan, add enough water to cover, and boil for about 5 minutes until just tender. Drain and cool slightly, then with the lid on, shake the pan lightly so that the potatoes dry and have a slight crumbling on the surface but retain their shape.

Place the oil, rosemary, salt and pepper in a bowl. Add the potatoes and parsnips and toss until well coated. Arrange the vegetables in a single layer in a baking tray. Bake for 1 hour, or until very crisp, adding garlic cloves after 30 minutes and turning occasionally. Serve immediately.

Potatoes Anna

I like to make this classic French buttery potato cake in a solid cast-iron frying pan, which can be put in the oven. Alternatively, a 20 cm cake tin can be used.

1 kg medium, yellow-fleshed potatoes,
    peeled and cut into wafer-thin slices
60 g butter
salt

SERVES 4–6

Preheat the oven to 190°C (375°F). Line a cast-iron frying pan or a 20 cm cake tin with baking paper. Place the potato slices in a colander and wash well under cold running water. Dry thoroughly with a tea towel. Place in a large bowl.

Melt the butter and toss in the potatoes with a large pinch of salt. Arrange potato slices in layers in the prepared pan or cake tin in neat overlapping circles. Bake for 30–45 minutes or until potatoes are tender and golden. Use a metal spatula or knife to lift and check the potatoes are not burning. Place a heated serving plate on top of the pan and flip over to turn out the potatoes. Serve hot.

ASPARAGUS

Although asparagus seems to be available most of the year, to many gourmets the first breath of spring is really when the best asparagus makes its appearance on the greengrocer's shelves. It is such a treat in our house, and we prepare this delicate vegetable with great respect. Asparagus can be served as an accompaniment, first course, in a stir-fry, vegetable platter or salad, warm or cold. I like it best when served simply and eaten with my fingers.

Cooking asparagus

Although you can buy special asparagus cookers, I find a wide, not-too-shallow frying pan with a lid is ideal.

To cook asparagus, first rinse the stalks thoroughly under a running tap to dislodge any grit. To trim, simply snap the spears near the base of each stem. When fresh, they should automatically disconnect just where tender meets tough. If necessary, use a potato peeler to remove any tough skin from the lower ends of the stalks. Tie into one or two bundles.

Cook the asparagus bundles in a saucepan of boiling salted water for 7–10 minutes or until tender, depending on the thickness of the stalks. Lift the asparagus from the water and lie on a clean, folded tea towel, undo the bundles and drain thoroughly. Allow 6–8 spears per person when serving as a separate course. Once you've cooked the asparagus, it can be finished in the following ways.

Baked Asparagus Bundles

Bundles of ham wrapped around asparagus and cheese make a good, simple lunch, brunch or supper — just serve with a loaf of crusty bread. Look for lovely fat asparagus spears.

15 g butter
4 spring onions, finely sliced
1 teaspoon Dijon mustard
6 tablespoons cream
a squeeze of lemon juice
250 g leg ham, thinly sliced
½ cup freshly grated parmesan cheese
2–3 bundles asparagus, cooked
freshly ground black pepper

SERVES 4

Preheat the oven to 190°C (375°F). Melt the butter in a small frying pan, add the spring onions and sauté until soft. Stir in the mustard, 2 tablespoons of the cream and the lemon juice and combine well.

Spread a small amount of the spring onion mixture evenly over each slice of ham. Sprinkle each with some parmesan.

Place two or three asparagus spears (depending on the size) in the centre of each ham slice. Fold the ham over the asparagus, and arrange the packages in a lightly greased baking dish. Pour over the remaining cream and sprinkle with remaining cheese and a good grinding of pepper. Bake for 15 minutes or until golden.

Asparagus Polonaise

A Polish way with asparagus: chopped hard-boiled eggs with parsley and fried breadcrumbs to give a lovely crunchy finish. This is a good way of changing the look of asparagus.

3 hard-boiled eggs, chopped
1 tablespoon chopped flat-leaf parsley
45 g butter
¾ cup fresh breadcrumbs
2–3 bundles asparagus, cooked

SERVES 4

Mix the hard-boiled eggs with the parsley. Heat the butter and fry breadcrumbs until golden. Stir in the eggs and parsley. Arrange the asparagus on a serving dish and spoon over the egg and breadcrumb mixture.

Flemish Asparagus

A recipe from northern France. As for many recipes with the name Flemish, the indication is that eggs will feature in the dish.

125 g butter
4 eggs, at room temperature
2–3 bundles asparagus, cooked

SERVES 4

Melt the butter and pour into 4 small ramekins. Soft-boil the eggs by lowering them into gently simmering water and leaving over a low heat for 2½ minutes. Put each egg in an eggcup. To serve, set out 4 plates and place about half a bundle of asparagus on each, with a ramekin of butter and an egg in an eggcup on the side. First dip an asparagus spear into the butter, then into the runny egg yolk, just as children do with 'toast soldiers'.

Asparagus Parmigiana

The simplest, yet most unusual way of serving asparagus comes from Italy.

2–3 bundles asparagus, cooked
¼–⅓ cup freshly grated parmesan cheese
75 g butter, melted
freshly ground black pepper

SERVES 4

Place the asparagus spears in a buttered ovenproof dish and sprinkle with the grated parmesan. Pour over the melted butter and season the lot with pepper.

Place under a grill or in the oven until the cheese has melted. Serve immediately.

Asparagus with Lemon Butter

Another simple way to cook asparagus that is delicious.

30 g butter
a squeeze of lemon juice
freshly ground black pepper
2–3 bundles asparagus, cooked

SERVES 4

Melt the butter and add a squeeze of lemon juice and a grinding of pepper. Arrange the hot asparagus on a serving dish and spoon lemon butter over the tips.

A SYMPHONY OF VEGETABLES

A love of vegetables is virtually a passport to good health. For many people, including me, vegetables never play second fiddle to other foods. Each day there's some new vegetable to discover and try.

Vegetables are wonderfully versatile. They can be stir-fried and served crisp with oriental seasonings or they can be steamed, preserving their natural flavour, colour and shape. Vegetables can be cooked in interesting combinations: braised in a frying pan or casserole dish, dressed with a variety of sauces or grilled to make a stunning platter for a party. In soups, stews, casseroles or salads, they add colour, flavour and nutrients.

Aim for garden-fresh flavour and texture, a vegetable's most appealing qualities. Choose a combination of vegetables, aiming for a variety of colours as well as tastes and textures.

Steamed vegetables

A collapsible steamer is a worthwhile investment because it allows the cooking of a wide variety of vegetables at one time. Steaming is perfect for baby vegetables.

Simply prepare the vegetables as usual and place them in a steamer over boiling water and cover with a lid. There should be sufficient room between the water and the food for the steam to develop and rise up through the vegetables. Start with the firmest vegetables at the bottom, and add the softer ones progressively, according to the cooking time.

As a guide, small new potatoes take about 15 minutes, young baby carrots and beans take about 8 minutes and halved patty-pan squash, zucchini, snow peas or English spinach take about 5 minutes.

When cooked, toss vegetables with a dab of butter, a squeeze of lemon juice or a sprinkle of chopped herbs, and finish with black pepper.

Grilled vegetables

Just about any vegetable can be grilled: eggplant, squash, mushrooms or young artichokes, to name a few. Most vegetables grill to perfection if halved or sliced, brushed with oil and cooked over a medium heat.

Grilled Vegetable Platter

Grilled vegetables make a delicious accompaniment to grilled meats, or can be served on their own with crusty bread for a light meal.

½–1 cup olive oil
1 teaspoon freshly ground black pepper
  or dried chilli flakes
¼ cup wine vinegar
200 g button squash, trimmed and halved
1 red onion, quartered lengthwise
1 head garlic, halved crosswise
½ punnet cherry tomatoes
1 bundle asparagus, tough stalk ends snapped off
2 long red or green chillies, halved and seeded
sea salt and freshly ground black pepper
a good squeeze of lemon juice
lemon wedges for serving

HERB SAUCE

1½ cups thick natural yoghurt
2 cloves garlic (optional)
4 tablespoons freshly chopped herbs such
  as flat-leaf parsley, basil or chives
salt and freshly ground black pepper

SERVES 6

In a large bowl, whisk the oil, pepper or chilli flakes, and vinegar. Add the squash, red onion, garlic, tomatoes, asparagus and chillies and toss gently. Marinate at room temperature for 1 hour.

Prepare a charcoal grill. Remove vegetables from the marinade and arrange them on the grill over medium–hot coals. Cook about 10 cm above the source of the heat. Alternatively, you can grill the vegetables under a very hot grill or preheated grill pan. Start on a high heat, then reduce heat for gentler cooking.

Grill the vegetables, turning once and brushing with oil as they cook, until coloured and tender. They should be lightly charred. Keep on a plate in a warm place until all are cooked. Drizzle with a little extra oil and season with sea salt, pepper and a good squeeze of lemon juice. Serve with lemon wedges and herb sauce or mayonnaise (page 232) on the side.

To prepare the herb sauce, combine all ingredients and mix well just before serving.

NOTE ~ Mushrooms, capsicums, eggplants and small leeks can also be grilled and added to your vegetable platter.

Trim the leeks, removing the tough outer skins, and make a vertical slit down the length of each, starting about 5 cm from the root end. Open out to allow easy washing to remove grit.

Aromatic Steamed Vegetables

There's nothing more welcome with a rich meal than lots of steamed vegetables, dressed with herbs and a drizzle of good-quality olive oil. Nutritionists agree this is the way to go — choose any vegetables in season.

10 asparagus spears or green beans
10 baby carrots or 2 carrots (cut into sticks)
8 broccoli or cauliflower
8 patty-pan squash
a sprig of thyme or oregano
a pinch of sea salt
3 tablespoons chopped fresh herbs such
   as flat-leaf parsley, chives, basil or chervil
freshly ground black pepper
1 tablespoon extra-virgin olive oil or butter

SERVES 6

Prepare the vegetables. Break the tough ends off the asparagus. Top the beans. Trim and wash the baby carrots if using. Trim any thick base stalks from the broccoli or cauliflower, and separate the heads into florets. Wash the squash and lightly trim the stem and end. Leave whole, or halve if large.

Put about 1½ cups of water in the base of a steamer and bring to the boil. Lay a sprig of thyme or oregano in the top. Arrange vegetables on top and salt lightly. Cover and steam for 5–8 minutes. Arrange vegetables on a serving plate or bowl and sprinkle generously with the herbs and pepper. Drizzle over olive oil or toss with butter.

Caesar Salad

Caesar salad has undergone a revival in Australian restaurants of late but sadly few versions resemble the original. There are many variations, but just as copies of luxury items, such as fake Hermès bags and Rolex watches, are poor imitations of the real thing, so it is the same for the Caesar salad. I believe this is the original recipe, created by Alexander Cardini when he was working as chef at the San Diego racetrack.

It was first prepared for me by Alexander Cardini Junior at his restaurant in Mexico City. I watched him carefully to be sure of capturing every detail of this simple but sophisticated dish. Noting my interest, he asked, 'Would you like to meet the man responsible for the Caesar salad?' The following day he took me to meet an elderly Mexican, his father, who told me he had created the salad in the 1920s in honour of his brother Caesar.

1 cos lettuce
4 anchovy fillets
1 clove garlic, crushed
2 tablespoons soft butter
8 slices baguette
1 teaspoon lemon juice
3 tablespoons olive oil
1 teaspoon Worcestershire sauce
a dash or 2 of Tabasco sauce
salt and freshly ground black pepper
1 large egg
3 tablespoons grated parmesan cheese

**SERVES 2 AS A LIGHT MEAL
OR 4 AS A FIRST COURSE**

Wash and dry the lettuce leaves, wrap in a tea towel and leave in the refrigerator to crisp. Preheat the oven to 180°C (350°F). Make croutons by mashing the anchovy fillets with garlic and butter and spreading on the bread slices. Place on a baking tray and bake for 10–15 minutes or until crisp. Leave to cool. Beat the lemon juice, oil, Worcestershire and Tabasco sauces together and set aside.

Arrange the lettuce leaves in a large salad bowl and season with salt and pepper. Coddle the egg by placing in boiling water for 50 seconds, then remove. Break egg over lettuce leaves, scooping out any egg clinging to the shell, and pour over the lemon and oil mixture, tossing lightly. Add croutons and grated cheese and gently roll salad in the dressing until each leaf glistens and the egg has formed part of the dressing. Serve immediately.

Niçoise Salad

I first came across this salad in 1955 when I was invited to lunch by my boss's French wife. We had lunch in her pretty sunroom and the first course was a simple and delicious niçoise salad.

Later I spent a few weeks in Provence and ate niçoise salad almost daily. I never tired of it; each day it was slightly different, depending on what the cook had on hand. Like all good salads, it is hard to ruin and usually delicious whatever the combination of ingredients, as long as they are fresh.

From its humble beginnings in the family kitchens of Nice, niçoise salad is now found on restaurant menus in every village in Provence, and many around the world.

500 g tuna steaks or 2 x 200 g cans tuna in oil
light olive oil
lemony herbs such as lemon thyme, lemon
 balm and citrus leaves
500 g new potatoes, scrubbed
4 large eggs, at room temperature
500 g green beans, topped and tailed
1 cos lettuce or bunch of English spinach,
 washed and dried
3 tomatoes, each cut into eighths
½ cup black olives (preferably kalamata)
chopped flat-leaf parsley, to garnish

VINAIGRETTE DRESSING

1 tablespoon Dijon mustard
salt and freshly ground black pepper
1 clove garlic, crushed
1 tablespoon chopped herbs such as
 flat-leaf parsley, chives or oregano
2 tablespoons white wine vinegar
2 teaspoons tarragon vinegar
1 tablespoon lemon juice
⅓ cup olive oil

SERVES 6

Place the tuna steaks (if using) in a snugly fitting ovenproof pan. Cover with light olive oil and add a few lemony herbs. Cover with foil and bake in a 150°C (300°F) oven for about 30 minutes. Remove from the oven and leave to cool in the oil.

Put the potatoes in a saucepan and cover with boiling water. Add a little salt and bring to the boil. Cook, uncovered, until the potatoes are tender, then drain. Lower the eggs carefully into warm water and bring the water slowly to the boil, stirring all the time so as to centre the yolks. Once the water is simmering, cook for 5 minutes. Drain, lightly crack the shells and leave to cool completely in cold water. Drop the prepared beans into a little boiling salted water and cook until tender yet crisp. Drain immediately, refresh under cold water and drain again.

Remove the tuna from the oil. Cut into large chunks. Arrange the lettuce on the base of a platter. Slice the potatoes thickly and arrange on top of the leaves. Arrange the beans, tomatoes, olives and quartered shelled eggs, and top with slices of tuna. Garnish with parsley.

For the dressing, mix together the mustard, salt, pepper, garlic, herbs, vinegars and lemon juice. Beat in the olive oil slowly to ensure the dressing remains thick and amalgamated. Beat again before using. Drizzle over the salad.

Diced Moroccan Salad

Fresh salads precede most meals in Morocco and, like Italian antipasti, are designed to inspire the appetite and refresh the palate. In this dish, vegetables such as cucumber, rocket and radish are seasoned with lemon juice, olives and mint sprigs. Good olives and olive oil are always in evidence.

Here are two salads that make an inviting platter when served together, although a small salad of either is just as good.

4 red radishes, sliced or diced
2–3 Lebanese cucumbers, lightly
  peeled and diced
1 small red onion, thinly sliced or diced
salt
½ cup torn mint leaves
1½ cups baby rocket leaves
1 clove garlic, finely chopped
2 tablespoons lemon juice
3 tablespoons extra-virgin olive oil
freshly ground black pepper
2 vine-ripened tomatoes, diced
12 small black olives, pitted
a few mint sprigs, to garnish
lemon wedges for serving

SERVES 4–6

Sprinkle the radishes, cucumbers and onion with a little salt and leave to stand for 5 minutes in a salad bowl. Add the mint and rocket.

In a small bowl, mix the garlic with the lemon juice, olive oil and pepper and pour over the vegetables. Toss ingredients together, cover with plastic wrap and chill for up to 2 hours. Just before serving, stir in the tomatoes and olives. Garnish with mint sprigs and serve with lemon wedges.

Shredded Moroccan salad

Using the fine shredding blades of a mandoline or a fine julienne shredder, grate 1 carrot, 1 beetroot and ½ large white radish (daikon), keeping them in separate piles. Make small mounds of each vegetable on a platter, generously squeeze over lemon juice, drizzle with olive oil and sprinkle lightly with ground cumin. Serve with lemon or orange wedges.

Roasted Capsicum with Garlic and Capers

I've been preparing capsicum this way since the 1960s when, considering myself a bit of a bohemian, I was seduced by robust dishes with gutsy flavours, just as they were made in France, Italy and Spain. This dish takes me straight back to Italy where I first learnt how to blister capsicum over a flame to char and skin them. What a difference it makes: not only do they end up with a delicious smoky flavour but the slippery smooth texture is divine. A salad with capsicum prepared in the following way is an integral part of any antipasti table in Italy.

4 red capsicums
3 tablespoons oil
4 cloves garlic, finely chopped
2 ripe tomatoes, peeled and roughly chopped
salt and freshly ground black pepper
¼ cup baby capers or black olives, pitted

SERVES 6

Cut the capsicums into quarters, remove seeds and ribs, and char as described opposite. Cut the capsicum pieces into thick strips and place in a shallow bowl.

Heat the oil in a large frying pan over a medium heat, add the garlic and cook until it just begins to colour. Add the capsicum strips and tomatoes, season with salt and pepper and cook for 5 minutes.

Add the capers or olives, stir through and turn the mixture out into a serving dish. This is lovely served with chunks of crusty bread.

Sweet capsicum salad

Prepare capsicums as described above. In a food processor, process 2 garlic cloves with 2 ripe tomatoes and some salt until finely chopped. Add 1 teaspoon of sherry or balsamic vinegar and mix again. Slowly pour in 4 tablespoons of extra-virgin olive oil with the motor running until dressing thickens. Pour dressing over the capsicum strips and toss to coat. Garnish with freshly chopped parsley or snipped basil. Leave for several hours for the flavours to develop.

Grilled Red Capsicum with Olives and Capers

This rustic, simpler version of roasted capsicum is good as a warm salad, but equally enjoyable as an accompaniment to a grill or on a cheese or meat sandwich. I recommend making a double quantity of this dish and keeping it in the refrigerator for when you are making pasta — use it instead of a pasta sauce.

4 red capsicums
2 tablespoons olive oil
½ cup black olives (kalamata or niçoise), pitted
1 clove garlic, chopped
1 tablespoon baby capers, drained
a handful of herbs such as flat-leaf parsley,
    oregano, chives or basil, roughly chopped
salt and freshly ground black pepper
a dash of balsamic vinegar

SERVES 6

Cut the capsicums into quarters, remove seeds and ribs, and prepare as described below. Cut each quarter into two or three strips and place them in a shallow serving dish. Heat the olive oil, olives, garlic, capers and herbs, tossing lightly for only an instant.

Add salt and pepper to taste and a dash of balsamic vinegar and spoon over the capsicums. Cover and leave to stand for at least 30 minutes before serving.

CHARRING CAPSICUMS

Charring capsicums all in one go over a barbecue, or under a very hot grill, is best, giving them a quarter-turn each time one section is blackened (if charring whole). This can be done over a gas flame, but takes a long time. As each capsicum is done, pop it into a plastic bag and close tightly so the capsicum can continue steaming. This will help the skin come away for easier peeling. Once the charred capsicums have cooled enough to handle, use the back of a knife to scrape off most of the skin, and then rinse off in a bowl of water to remove any stubborn black bits.

Sicilian Caponata

When I worked as a writer for *Woman's Day*, I was invited to many countries eager to show me their culinary customs. Italy was one of my favourite destinations, and the Italian practice of using only the freshest vegetables was something that I was keen to write about. Even as a child I had been taught the importance of choosing the best. If I brought home a squashy tomato, my mother would tell me, 'Go back, Margaret, and learn to watch what you're doing.'

This zesty Italian dish of sweet and sour vegetables is great for picking up jaded appetites, particularly in summer. It can include sultanas, which add an extra sweetness, and can easily be doubled. You can skip peeling the tomatoes if you don't mind coming across a bit of skin. For a first course, serve at room temperature with crusty bread. For a lunch or light meal, serve with hard-boiled eggs, fried fish or grilled chicken.

1 medium eggplant
salt
⅓ cup olive oil
2 stalks celery, thinly sliced
1 onion, thinly sliced
2 tomatoes, peeled, seeded and diced
1 tablespoon drained capers
1 tablespoon pine nuts (optional)
a handful of black or green olives
1 tablespoon sugar
2 tablespoons wine vinegar
freshly ground black pepper

SERVES 4–6

Cut the eggplant into small cubes, sprinkle with salt and leave to drain for 30 minutes. Heat half the oil in a deep frying pan and fry the cubes a few at a time until browned and soft, adding a little more oil as necessary.

Return all eggplant to the pan with the celery, onion and tomatoes. Simmer for 15–20 minutes and then add the capers, pine nuts (if using) and olives. Stir the sugar into the vinegar until dissolved and add to the pan. Season with salt and pepper and simmer very gently for a further 15 minutes. Taste and add a little more vinegar if necessary. Store covered in the refrigerator and serve with crusty bread.

TIP – The flavour of the caponata improves greatly if made a day or two ahead. It can be served warm or at room temperature, and on its own or with plenty of crusty bread. Caponata can be eaten as an hors d'oeuvre, as you would a dip, or in larger servings as a light meal. I love it with a piece of grilled fish, a lamb cutlet or a hard-boiled egg.

Seafood and Pasta Salad

If you live in Sydney on the beautiful harbour as I do, you will know how exciting it is to enjoy a sunny day on the deck with friends, relaxing, eating, drinking, enjoying lively conversation and watching the passing boats. For years now I have risen early on a Sunday morning and headed for the fish markets. As I have never been big on barbecues, what I have become good at is preparing fresh seafood, cooking and combining it with pasta and a great dressing, then serving it all with a loaf of crusty bread and a glass of crisp wine.

This seafood and pasta salad changes from time to time, depending on what is available at the fish markets. When I'm very busy, I often buy the seafood ready prepared or make a similar salad of pasta, canned fish such as tuna, hard-boiled eggs, anchovies, black olives and greens. The essence of this dish lies in the freshness of the seafood and the quality of the pasta.

500 g green (raw) or cooked prawns,
   shelled and deveined
250 g scallops
500 g small mussels
400 g small calamari tubes
1 teaspoon grated lemon rind
1–2 tablespoons lemon juice
salt and freshly ground black pepper
2 teaspoons snipped chives
1 teaspoon Dijon mustard
1 tablespoon finely chopped tarragon
   or roughly torn basil leaves
½ cup light olive oil
500 g fresh green tagliatelle, linguine
   or fettuccine
1 tablespoon olive oil
250 g snow peas or asparagus tips, lightly
   cooked and cooled
1 small red chilli, thinly sliced
3 tablespoons chopped herbs such as flat-leaf
   parsley, basil, chives or chervil, to garnish

SERVES 6–8

Prepare and cook the fresh seafood (see opposite). Combine the cooked seafood in a large bowl. In the bowl of a food processor, process the lemon rind and juice, salt and pepper, chives, mustard and tarragon or basil until well mixed. With the motor still running, gradually add the olive oil in a slow, steady stream to make a thick creamy dressing. Add 3 tablespoons of the dressing to the seafood and toss.

Cook the pasta in a large pot of boiling salted water until al dente, which means firm to the bite, then drain thoroughly. While still warm toss through the tablespoon of oil with forks or by hand.

Toss the pasta with the seafood — reserving some seafood for the garnish — snow peas or asparagus and remaining dressing. Turn onto a serving platter and garnish with slivers of red chilli and the reserved seafood. Garnish with chopped herbs.

TO PREPARE AND COOK THE SEAFOOD

If using green (raw) prawns, drop them into a large pot of boiling salted water on high heat. Stir until the prawns take on a pink tinge, then reduce heat to medium, cover and simmer for 2 minutes. Drain, shell and devein the prawns. The tails can be left on for decorative effect.

To cook scallops, rinse and remove any brown bits, then poach gently in salted water for about 2 minutes. Drain and cool.

Scrub mussels thoroughly in plenty of water, tug off any seaweed and beards and rinse thoroughly. If possible, leave them to soak for an hour or so in cold water, enough to cover. Then place the mussels in a large saucepan with ½ cup of water over a high heat and steam, covered, shaking the pan occasionally, for 4–6 minutes or until the shells have opened. The moment they are all open put the pan aside to cool a little. When cool enough remove the mussels from their shells.

To prepare calamari, squeeze out the ink and quills from the tubes and wash the calamari very thoroughly in cold water. Drain and pat dry with paper towels. Cut the flaps and tentacles from the tubes and slice the tubes into thin rings. Trim the base of the tentacles from the heads and wash. Pat the rings, flaps and tentacles dry with paper towels. Heat 1–2 tablespoons of oil in a heavy-based frying pan and when very hot quickly sauté the calamari for a few minutes, until the colour just changes.

Snapper and Mayonnaise Salad

Inspired by holidays in Greece, this snapper and mayonnaise salad is a fabulous-looking dish for summer buffets. Shape in a ring mould or save the head and tail and re-shape as a whole fish. It's the ideal dish for a gathering as guests can serve themselves easily while chatting.

1 large snapper or other firm white fish,
    weighing 1.5–2 kg, cleaned
juice of 1 lemon
salt and freshly ground black pepper
1 cup dry white wine
1 cup sliced tender young celery
¼ cup snipped dill and chives
¼ cup chopped flat-leaf parsley
Mayonnaise (page 232)
slices of cucumber, sprigs of dill and lemon
    slices, to garnish

**SERVES 8-10 OR MORE AS PART OF
A BUFFET**

Preheat the oven to 180°C (350°F). Wipe the fish inside and out with paper towels. Sprinkle with the lemon juice and season with salt and a good grinding of pepper. Place in a large baking dish.

Pour the wine over and around and cover with a sheet of baking paper or lightly oiled aluminium foil. Bake for about 35 minutes or until the flesh flakes easily when tested with a fork.

Remove the fish from the oven and leave to cool in the dish. Strain off the cooking liquid and reserve in the refrigerator. Remove the head and tail by cutting across with a good sharp knife or scissors. Save them for finishing the dish.

Remove the skin and bones from the rest of the fish and break the flesh into pieces, putting the prepared fish in a bowl as you work. Now fold through the celery, dill, chives and parsley, plus enough mayonnaise to bind the mixture, and season well, adding plenty of salt and pepper to taste.

Spoon into a lightly oiled ring tin or arrange the head and tail at each end of a serving platter and spoon the fish salad between, arranging and smoothing so that it resembles the shape of the fish. If using a ring tin, carefully turn out onto a large platter. With a small metal spatula smooth the surface evenly and garnish the centre with slices of cucumber, sprigs of dill and lemon slices. Cover lightly and refrigerate until ready to serve. Stir 2 or 3 tablespoons of the reserved cooking liquid into 1 cup of mayonnaise and use it as a sauce to accompany the fish.

Sichuan Chicken Salad

Sichuan is the western school of richly flavoured and piquant Chinese food. Every dish in a Chinese meal should include two or more textures: tenderness, crispness, crunchiness, smoothness and softness. In this salad, the chicken is white and tender, the celery is crisp and pale green, the spring onions and coriander leaves are a rich dark green, and a colourful chopped chilli provides heat and flecks of red throughout the salad. The addition of soy sauce, sesame oil and Sichuan pepper, with its distinctive fragrance and curious numbing effect on the tongue, makes this dish unique.

300 g boned breast of Chinese White Chicken (page 92), skinned, or poached chicken breasts (see Tip)
1 Lebanese cucumber
4 spring onions, cut into thin julienne
½ cup roughly chopped coriander leaves
1 cup celery, cut into thin matchsticks
1½ tablespoons light soy sauce
1 teaspoon sesame oil
1 teaspoon dried chilli flakes or 1 chilli, seeded and diced
½ teaspoon coarsely ground Sichuan pepper, plus a little extra, to garnish

SERVES 2 AS A MAIN COURSE, 4 AS AN APPETISER

Shred the chicken breast with your fingers, tearing into long strips. Set aside. With a vegetable peeler, peel the cucumber lightly, leaving the green flesh on the outside surface intact. Cut lengthwise into thin slices, then cut into thin julienne strips. In a bowl, combine the chicken with the cucumber and remaining ingredients. Pile on a serving plate sprinkled with extra Sichuan pepper and a little salt.

TIP ~ To poach chicken, combine the following in a saucepan: 2 cups of water, 1 teaspoon of salt, 2 chopped spring onions, ½ celery stalk and ½ carrot, both chopped. Bring slowly to the boil. Add 3 half-breasts of chicken, bring back to the boil, reduce heat, cover and simmer for 8–10 minutes. Place the chicken in a container, strain liquor over the chicken, cover and allow to cool. Refrigerate and use as required. If you prefer dark meat, chicken thighs may be treated the same way.

Hot Thai Beef Salad

Whenever I travel to Europe these days I find myself missing the food back home! Not just the simple food, such as a sandwich made with sourdough bread and an ox-heart tomato, but the Asian food that we can so easily make at home or eat in restaurants. I've become hooked on Chinese, Vietnamese, Malaysian and Thai food not only because I love the flavours, but also because the ingredients are affordable and easily obtained. I was introduced to the wonders of Thai food more than 20 years ago through Bupah, a friend of Suzanne's. She taught us to make Thai fish cakes, a quick beef, chicken or fish curry using prepared curry paste, and this hot Thai beef salad.

500 g rump or sirloin steak
  freshly ground black pepper
½ cup torn mint leaves
1 large red onion or 2 large spring onions,
  thinly sliced
2 red chillies, sliced
juice of 1 large lime or ½ lemon
2 tablespoons fish sauce
1 teaspoon sugar
a handful of mixed salad greens
1 cup cherry tomatoes
a handful of rice vermicelli (see Note overleaf)
vegetable oil for frying
2 tablespoons roughly chopped roasted peanuts
1 red chilli, halved
lime wedges for serving

SERVES 4-6

Season the steak with pepper and cook on a hot ribbed grill or under a preheated grill for 5 minutes on each side or until done to taste. Remove and leave to stand for 10 minutes. Cut steak into very thin slices and place in a bowl with any meat juices. Meanwhile, combine the mint leaves with the onions, chillies, lime or lemon juice, fish sauce and sugar. Stir well and add to the beef slices, tossing. Combine with the mixed salad greens and cherry tomatoes and set aside.

Heat some vegetable oil in a wok, testing the heat with a few strands of vermicelli. It should swell immediately if the oil is hot enough. Fry the vermicelli, scooping out with a wire strainer as soon as they puff and turn pale golden. Drain well on paper towels and cool, then arrange in a bowl.

Pile the beef salad on top of the crispy noodles. Scatter with peanuts and chilli and serve with lime wedges. >>

NOTE ~ You'll find vermicelli at Asian food stores or supermarkets. There are two kinds: rice vermicelli or mung bean vermicelli (also known as glass, cellophane or transparent noodles). Mung bean vermicelli are made of flour and have a soft, slippery texture; rice vermicelli are firmer and whiter when cooked and are mostly used in fresh spring rolls, laksa and Vietnamese dishes. You can make the salad using either one.

TO PREPARE MUNG BEAN VERMICELLI

Soak 100 g of mung bean vermicelli in hot water for 10 minutes, stirring to ensure that strands do not clump together. If not tender, drain, return to the bowl and add more hot water, soaking again until tender. Drain and refresh under cold water, then drain again. Arrange the drained vermicelli on a serving platter and top with the beef salad. Scatter with peanuts and red chilli and serve with lime wedges.

Thai Pork Salad

'What are they having?' How often have you heard that question in a restaurant as someone points to another table? That's the way many of us learn to try a new dish, particularly if it is a cuisine with which we are not wholly familiar. That's how I discovered Thai pork salad. A large bowl of crisp lettuce cups and a dish of fresh-looking salad were taken to another table. The diners quickly spooned the salad into the lettuce cups, deftly wrapping the lettuce leaves around the filling to make a neat package and eating it with their hands. Steaming hot towelling napkins were offered for wiping fingers, but a finger bowl with water and a lemon slice does the same job.

500 g lean pork, finely chopped or minced
3 tablespoons water
2 tablespoons lemon juice
2 tablespoons Thai fish sauce
½ teaspoon finely sliced chilli
2 tablespoons roasted peanuts, skinned
1 red or salad onion, finely sliced
6–8 spring onions, cut into short lengths
2 tablespoons finely shredded fresh ginger
6–8 mint leaves
½ cup torn fresh coriander leaves
8 or more crisp lettuce cups (iceberg lettuce
   is ideal)

SERVES 4–6

Cook the pork in the water in a wok over a medium heat, stirring to prevent lumps from forming, until the pork is tender. Transfer to a bowl to cool. Add the lemon juice and all other ingredients except the lettuce leaves, and toss lightly.

Spoon the pork mixture into the lettuce cups. Wrap the lettuce cups around the pork and eat with your hands.

Desserts

Ricotta Pancakes with Fig Jam and Cream

Many years ago when I was giving cookery lessons at Johnny Walker's Sydney bistro, we had someone make little cast-iron crêpe pans. They were only 18 centimetres in diameter, with five millimetre straight sides that made turning pancakes and crêpes much easier. We recommended purchasing two at a time to help speed up the making of crêpes. I still treasure mine. You can buy good non-stick omelette pans today, but make sure they are heavy so that the crêpes don't burn.

These pancakes make a special breakfast or dessert. As with sandwiches, pancakes offer a field day for the creative cook to add imaginative touches; for example, figs that have been sugared and lightly grilled could replace the fig jam, as could lightly sugared berries.

250 g ricotta
2 tablespoons caster sugar
1 egg
1 cup milk
1 cup self-raising flour
20 g butter, melted
fig jam and whipped cream, for serving

MAKES 10

Whisk the ricotta, sugar and egg together in a bowl. Stir in the milk, then the flour until well combined. Pour batter into a jug.

Brush a non-stick frying pan with some melted butter over a medium heat. While tilting the pan, pour in enough batter to make a 12-cm pancake. Cook until bubbles appear on surface, about 2 minutes, then flip over using a metal spatula and cook until golden. Stack pancakes and keep warm. Wipe the pan with paper towel and cook remaining batter.

Serve the pancakes warm with fig jam and whipped cream.

TIP ~ Because these pancakes are made with self-raising flour there's no need to let the batter stand before cooking. That would cause the raising agent to fizz out, making the pancakes heavier. A plain-flour batter needs to stand for around 30 minutes so that the starch cells have time to swell with the moisture. They will then burst on contact with the heat, making the pancakes light and fluffy.

Pikelets

When fellow Scot Sue Lawrence came to Australia to launch her prize-winning book *Scots Cooking*, she shocked the manager of a cooking school by requesting a girdle. She didn't mean something you buy in a lingerie shop — she meant a Scottish girdle for making potato scones and drop scones, which are also known as Scotch pancakes or, here in Australia, pikelets. 'Margaret Fulton is bound to have one,' she told the manager, and was right. I had helped design one for a well-known saucepan company and I endorsed it with my name on the base. Sue thought it was the best girdle she'd ever used.

As Sue says, 'This is fast food as it was meant to be. From mixing the ingredients to eating, these pikelets take just 10 minutes.'

1 cup self-raising flour
½ teaspoon salt
2 tablespoons sugar
1 egg, beaten
1 cup milk or buttermilk
30 g butter, melted
a little extra butter, for cooking

MAKES 12–15

Sift the flour and salt into a bowl. Stir in the sugar and make a well in the centre. Mix together the egg, milk and butter. Pour the egg mixture into the well and, using a wooden spoon, gradually draw in the flour until you have a smooth batter.

Heat a little butter in a girdle or a large heavy-based frying pan. Test the mixture by dropping 1 tablespoon into the pan. If it doesn't drop easily the mixture may need more milk. Drop the batter by the tablespoon into the pan and cook pikelets over a medium heat until the bottoms are golden and the tops covered with bubbles. This should take just 1½–2 minutes. Turn carefully and cook the other side. Remove and keep warm in a folded tea towel while you cook the rest of the batter, adding more butter to the pan if necessary. Serve warm with butter and honey or a good berry jam and a spoonful of whipped cream.

Fruit pikelets

Add ⅓ cup of seedless raisins or sultanas to the batter and stir in 1 tablespoon of golden syrup in place of the sugar.

NOTE - Pikelets can be reheated briefly in a warm oven or under a slow grill.

Lemon Honeycomb Mould

A lemon tree is a must in every cook's garden and this old-fashioned dessert has a clean, sharp taste that is so refreshing, especially during summer. The mould should have three distinct layers: a cap of clear lemon jelly, a thin band of opaque cream jelly and a spongy base (the honeycomb), which makes a cracking noise when eaten.

1 tablespoon powdered gelatine
4 tablespoons water
2 eggs, separated
⅓ cup caster sugar
finely grated rind and juice of 2 lemons
1¼ cups milk

SERVES 6

Lightly oil a 900 ml fluted mould. Sprinkle the gelatine over the water in a small bowl and leave to soften for 5 minutes. In a bowl, whisk together the egg yolks with the sugar and lemon rind.

Bring the milk to the boil and pour over the egg yolk mixture, whisking constantly. Return to the saucepan and cook, stirring, over a gentle heat until the custard thickens and coats the back of a spoon. Do not allow to boil. Remove from the heat and stir in the gelatine until completely dissolved. Add the lemon juice.

Whisk the egg whites until stiff but not dry and fold into the mixture with a large spoon. Pour into the mould and chill until set. Turn out onto a serving plate to serve.

Crème Caramel

This recipe for delicious little custard desserts created a sensation way back in 1968 when I included it in my first cookbook. People loved it but many wrote to say the toffee caramel stayed in the bottom of the moulds. Pretty soon everyone understood that the caramel flavoured the rich custard and gave it a lovely colour when turned out. The longer it is left in the fridge (overnight at least), the more caramel sauce you have. Some recipes call for cream only but to my mind the addition of milk, to cut down on the richness, gives a perfect result.

Cook the caramel to just the right stage: not enough and it will be over-sweet, too much and it will be bitter. Use a sugar thermometer or learn to recognise the caramel stage by using your nose and eyes. Once the caramel stage is reached it will burn quickly and you will smell the bitterness. Therefore it is important to work quickly, pouring the caramel into the moulds as soon as it is ready. Start again if it burns so as not to waste the custard mixture.

½ cup water
1 cup sugar
1 cup cream
1½ cups milk
1 vanilla bean
3 eggs
2 egg yolks
½ cup extra caster sugar

SERVES 6

Preheat the oven to 160ºC (320ºF). Put the water and sugar in a small saucepan over a low heat until the sugar dissolves. Increase the heat and boil until golden brown (caramel stage). Pour into an 18 cm mould or 6 individual moulds. Hold the mould with a cloth and quickly rotate until the caramel coats the sides and base. If using individual moulds, pour a little caramel into the base of each. Leave to cool.

Scald the cream and milk with the vanilla bean. Strain and cool slightly. Whisk the eggs, egg yolks and extra sugar until well blended, then pour in the milk gradually, stirring constantly. Strain through a fine sieve.

Pour the custard mixture into the caramel-lined mould or individual moulds and place in a baking dish filled with hot water that reaches halfway up the sides of the moulds. Bake small moulds for 45 minutes, a large mould for 50–60 minutes, or until custard is set and a skewer inserted near the centre comes out clean. Cool, then chill in the refrigerator for several hours or overnight. Turn out onto serving plates. Serve with cream. >>

Cardamom cream

When I joined *New Idea* in 1979 I was given plenty of time to create new recipe ideas. In 1980 I developed a rich cream flavoured with one of my favourite spices, cardamom. It's a variation of crème caramel, made in the same way except that the cream and milk are infused with 8 crushed cardamom pods instead of the vanilla bean.

Crème peruvienne

Another variation, in which the milk and cream are infused with fresh coffee beans. Replace the vanilla bean with 1 cup of lightly crushed coffee beans. Leave to infuse for 10 minutes, covered. Strain through a fine sieve and proceed as per the original recipe.

The Spanish and French 'flan' is made the same way but in a larger mould, and often evaporated milk is used in place of milk and cream.

Vanilla Sugar

Vanilla sugar is fabulous for sprinkling over fruits and for cooking cakes and biscuits. It also makes a great gift.

vanilla beans, broken
into pieces
granulated sugar

To make, simply place one or as many vanilla beans as you can spare in a blender. Add granulated sugar to capacity and whiz on and off until the bean has been processed through the sugar, giving it an ashy look. Store immediately in glass jars with lids or in a sugar canister.

Vanilla Kippels (Kipferls)

Vanilla kippels, or kipferls, as they are known in Germany and Austria, are usually made at Christmas. They can be made with different nuts, such as walnuts or almonds, although in Bavaria it is nearly always hazelnuts. Care should be taken to process the nuts to a meal without letting them become a paste. There should be little pieces of nut recognisable in the mixture. The vanilla taste is also important. Store the biscuits in a glass jar together with a piece of vanilla bean — they make a lovely gift when presented in this way and will keep for several weeks.

100 g walnuts, almonds or hazelnuts
125 g butter, softened
¼ cup caster sugar
½ teaspoon vanilla essence
1¼ cups plain flour
a pinch of salt
Vanilla Sugar (page opposite) or sifted icing
    sugar for dusting

MAKES ABOUT 40

Preheat the oven to 180°C (350°F). Butter 2 baking trays. Using the pulse button, process nuts in a food processor until finely chopped or coarsely ground.

Use an electric beater to cream the butter with the sugar and vanilla until the mixture is light and fluffy. Sift the flour with the salt and fold into the creamed mixture along with the walnuts. Lightly mix to form a dough. If the mixture is too sticky, add a little more flour.

Pinch off small pieces of dough and roll into walnut-size balls. Roll each ball in the palm of the hand to form a small tube, then curve gently into a crescent. Arrange on the prepared baking trays.

Bake for 20–25 minutes, until lightly coloured. Transfer the biscuits to a wire rack over a sheet of greaseproof paper. Dredge the kippels lightly with vanilla sugar or sifted icing sugar while they are still warm. Cool and store in an airtight container.

NOTE ~ In warmer weather the dough may be a little tricky to handle. In this case, knead lightly until smooth and then form into a ball. Wrap in plastic wrap and chill for 1 hour.

Brandy Snaps

Crunchy, crisp brandy snaps have been made for centuries in Britain, where they were often given as gifts by vendors at medieval fairs, along with gingerbreads and hokey pokey. Later they became an afternoon tea treat, filled with whipped cream.

Shape them into tubes with the help of a wooden spoon, into curls with a rolling pin, or flick them onto an upturned glass to shape them into baskets for filling with cream and fruits, or a mousse mixture. There's a little skill involved in timing the baking, so that the biscuits don't stick to the trays, and rolling gently and quickly to shape them. They must be kept in an airtight container once cooled.

80 g butter
4 tablespoons caster or brown sugar
4 tablespoons golden syrup
½ cup plain flour, sifted
1 teaspoon ground ginger
grated rind of ½ lemon
whipped cream for filling (optional)

MAKES 20

Preheat the oven to 180ºC (350ºF). Grease 2 baking trays and the round handles of 2 wooden spoons (the larger the better). Put the butter, sugar and golden syrup into a pan and heat gently until butter has melted. Remove from the heat and cool until lukewarm. Stir in the sifted flour with the ginger and lemon rind.

Make 3 snaps at a time. Place a teaspoon of mixture on a tray for each, allowing room for spreading. Using a metal spatula spread to 8 cm in diameter and bake for 5–8 minutes. When golden brown, remove from the oven, stand for a minute or so until set a little, then ease from the tray with a broad-bladed knife or metal spatula. Working quickly, wrap each one lightly around the greased wooden-spoon handle, keeping the smooth side of the biscuit to the handle of the spoon. Before completely set, slip off onto a rack to cool. Continue with remaining mixture, alternating trays. One tray should be in the oven while you are curling the snaps from the tray already cooked. Keep in an airtight container until ready to fill and serve.

An hour or two before serving, pipe whipped cream (if using) into each end of the snaps.

Meringues

Gasparini, a Swiss pastry cook from the town of Meiringen in Switzerland, was expecting a visit from Napoleon when he created a confection using nuts, sugar and egg yolks. Not wanting to waste the egg whites, he whipped them together with sugar and shaped them into mounds, which he baked until crisp and dry and served in saucers brimming with cream. It is said Napoleon preferred the second creation and named them after the town.

When Suzanne was the pastry chef at the Cordon Bleu Restaurant in London's Marylebone Lane, she kept tins of meringues in different shapes ready to make desserts, little cakes and petits fours at the drop of a hat. Her customers would queue down the street for them. Meringues are one of the most versatile offerings of the kitchen.

3 large egg whites
1 cup caster sugar
whipped cream, for filling (optional)

MAKES UP TO 50

Preheat the oven to 120°C (250°F). Brush several baking trays lightly with oil and dust with flour, or use baking paper to line the trays.

Using either a freshly cleaned copper bowl with a balloon whisk or the bowl of an electric mixer, beat the egg whites, slowly at first, until frothy. Start to beat quickly until the peaks hold their shape. Gradually beat in 2 tablespoons of the sugar and continue beating for 2–3 minutes. Add the remaining sugar and fold in lightly and quickly using a large metal spoon.

Pipe onto the prepared trays, or shape with two spoons (see opposite). Bake for 1½ hours. Ease the meringues from the trays, turn over and return to oven for a further 30 minutes or until crisp, dry and a delicate beige in colour. When cool, store in an airtight container.

The shells may be hollowed (see opposite) so that they can hold a fair proportion of whipped cream and the two halves will not slip when sandwiched together.

Piped meringue shells

Meringues may be made bite-sized for petits fours or egg-sized for dessert. Put the meringue mixture into a piping bag with a plain nozzle and pipe rounds, wider at the base and spiralling each one to a peak. When the meringues are set, gently press them underneath with your finger to form a hollow, return them to the trays on their sides and return to the oven for 20–30 minutes to allow the undersides to dry. Remove from the oven and cool. Store in an airtight container until needed.

Chocolate-coated meringue fingers

Put the meringue mixture into a piping bag and, using a plain nozzle, pipe small finger-lengths onto prepared baking trays. Bake until crisp and dry, then cool on wire racks for a few minutes. Store in an airtight container until required.

To chocolate-coat one end of the meringue, have ready a small bowl with a little chocolate that has been melted gently over hot water, and a saucer of finely chopped nuts. Dip either one or both ends of the cooked meringue fingers into the chocolate, then sprinkle lightly with the nuts. Return to the rack to set the chocolate.

SHAPING MERINGUES WITH SPOONS

To make pretty-shaped meringues, you will need two dessertspoons, a metal spatula or palette knife, and a jug of iced water.

Take a spoonful of the meringue mixture in a wet spoon and with a wet spatula quickly smooth it over, piling it in the centre and pointing the two ends to form a half-egg shape. With the second spoon, scoop the meringue out onto a prepared baking sheet. Leave a space of at least 2 cm between each meringue.

Bake until they are crisp and remove from the oven. Turn each meringue over, and then make a hollow indentation in each one by pressing underneath gently with your finger. Return to the oven for a little longer to dry completely.

Whip cream until thick and sweeten and flavour it if desired. Fill the meringue with the cream, putting two pieces of meringue together. Pile in paper cases on a glass or silver dish.

Demerara Meringues

Demerara sugar is the least refined sugar and still has much of the molasses left in the crystals, which gives it a distinctive, rich flavour. When used in making meringues, its flavour and texture make for a light meringue, pale bisque in colour. Dredging the tops of the unbaked meringue with a little Demerara adds a pretty, golden crystal finish. Demerara meringues go well with whipped cream and a chocolate or caramel sauce (page 221) on the side.

½ cup Demerara sugar
2 large egg whites

MAKES 12

Spread the sugar out on a baking tray and place in the oven at 100°C (210°F) for an hour or so to dry out. Leave to cool then place in a blender or food processor and grind the sugar fairly finely.

Beat the egg whites until they form soft peaks then beat in half the sugar until the mixture is thick and shiny. Using a large metal spoon, gently fold in the remaining sugar. To do this, cut gently down through the mixture and lift some up and over onto the top, repeating until whites and sugar are lightly mixed. It is not necessary to mix thoroughly; if the mixture is overworked the air cells in the meringue will break down.

To shape the meringues, use 2 wet dessertspoons. With one, scoop up a heaped spoonful of mixture. With the other spoon, scoop this mixture out onto a baking tray lined with baking paper, to form a half-egg shape. If necessary, neaten the shape with a knife dipped in cold water. Repeat until all mixture is used. This should make 12 meringues.

Dredge the tops with a little extra Demerara sugar and bake in a 120°C (250°F) oven for 1 hour or longer until firm. Gently lift each meringue off the tray, press the base with your finger while still warm to make a hollow and return to oven for a further 30 minutes until crisp and dry. Leave to cool in the turned-off oven.

Demerara Meringues with Chestnut and Chocolate

If you want to create a really impressive Demerara meringue dessert, go a few steps further and fill two meringues with a chestnut and chocolate purée and serve with thick cream. This is a delicious combination, and a truly sumptuous dessert.

1 quantity Demerara meringues (opposite)
¼ cup sugar
⅓ cup milk
⅓ cup canned unsweetened chestnut purée
60 g dark chocolate, chopped
½ cup cream
pieces of marrons glacés (poached chestnuts
    in syrup) or shavings of dark chocolate,
    to decorate

SERVES 6

First make the meringues and store in an airtight container until needed. Dissolve the sugar in the milk over a gentle heat. Add the chestnut purée and chocolate, and stir until smooth. If lumpy, rub through a sieve. Leave to cool completely.

Whip the cream and fold into the mixture. Spread a good scoop onto the base of one meringue. Top with another meringue and place on a plate. Scatter with pieces of marrons glacés and syrup or shaved chocolate. Serve with a dollop of thick cream.

NOTE ~ The secret to making crisp, light meringues is the timing. You must work quickly once the sugar is added or the meringue will wilt. Avoid rainy days or humid weather, and most importantly don't make them while doing other cooking — the moisture in the air will make the dried meringues weep. If the meringues should absorb any moisture, they can be dried in a very slow oven (100°C/210°F) for 15 minutes or so. When cooled, store in an airtight container.

Clean utensils are also essential. Fats, oils and grease, even a trace of egg yolk, will reduce the volume of your meringue. Also, ensure the egg whites are at room temperature — this maximises the air they will absorb when beaten.

Shape the meringue mixture into shells, crusts, baskets or all manner of fancy designs. They will keep for weeks, even months, in a clean, airtight jar or tin, ready at any time for myriad uses. Fill with cream, berries or any other soft fruits, finish with a fruit sauce or coulis, or fill or top with a piped rosette of chocolate, coffee or chestnut cream.

Pavlova

Pavlova, named after the Russian ballerina Anna Pavlova, is still just about the most popular party dessert in Australia. Everyone has their favourite texture, be it the crisp meringue shell or the delicate soft marshmallow. The following recipe was given to me by a churchgoer who won acclaim for her 'pavs' and made at least five a week for members of the congregation.

The meringue puffs up as light as a feather, looking just like Pavlova's tutu, and the tart-sweet flavour of the passionfruit and strawberries adds a distinctive flavour to the dessert.

6 egg whites, at room temperature
a pinch of salt
2 cups caster sugar
1½ teaspoons vinegar
1½ teaspoons vanilla essence
1¼ cups cream
pulp of 3 passionfruit
½ punnet strawberries, hulled and sliced

SERVES 8–10

Preheat the oven to 200–210°C (400–410°F). Place a piece of baking paper on a baking tray and mark a 23 cm circle on it to use as a guide (the pavlova will spread a little).

In an electric mixer, beat the egg whites and salt at full speed until they stand in stiff peaks. Sift the sugar and gradually sprinkle into the egg white mixture 1 tablespoon at a time, beating at high speed until all sugar has been added. Lastly, fold in the vinegar and vanilla. Spoon large dollops inside the circle on the baking sheet and smooth over the top lightly. Place in the oven (reducing heat to 150°C/300°F) for 1 hour. Turn off the heat and leave pavlova in the oven until cold. If using a gas oven bake at 150°C (300°F) for 1 hour, reduce heat to 120°C (250°F) for a further 30 minutes and then turn heat off and leave the pavlova in the oven until completely cooled.

When the pavlova is cooled, slide onto a large, flat cake plate, removing the baking paper. Don't worry if it collapses slightly; you should also expect cracks on the surface. Whip the cream until stiff but still shiny and spoon over the top of the pavlova. Spoon passionfruit and strawberries over the cream and serve. >>

Individual pavlovas

Preheat the oven to 180°C (350°F). Line a baking tray with baking paper and use a pencil to mark the paper with 6 x 7.5 cm circles. Whisk 3 egg whites at room temperature with a pinch of salt until they hold soft peaks. Add ⅔ cup of caster sugar, a little at a time, beating constantly. Beat in 1 teaspoon of vinegar and ¼ teaspoon of vanilla essence. The mixture should now hold stiff peaks.

Spread the meringue on the paper within the marked circles and bake for about 20 minutes or until pale golden. Leave in the turned-off oven to cool completely before carefully transferring to serving plates. Serve topped with whipped cream and fresh fruit.

Choice of fruit

Passionfruit and sliced strawberries are a good combination. A tablespoon of icing sugar may be added to sweeten them, if you like. Sliced strawberries macerated with a tablespoon of Kirsch or orange-flavoured liqueur is a delicious topping. A New Zealand favourite, sliced kiwifruit, adds a fresh flavour and colour.

Four-egg pavlova

For a smaller, family-size pavlova, use the basic recipe, reducing the number of egg whites to 4 and the sugar to 1½ cups. Otherwise, everything remains the same.

Pavlova in a springform tin

Cut a circle of baking paper to line the base of a 23 cm springform tin and brush the sides with oil. Pile the meringue mixture into the prepared tin and bake as per the basic recipe. When cool, release the sides of the tin, slide pavlova onto a flat plate and finish as per the basic recipe.

Rolled Pavlova

For those who love this light-as-air dessert, it's a miracle that it can take another form and still be so good. There won't be that crispy shell but there is lots of lovely soft marshmallowy meringue holding luscious filling. Its time in the refrigerator means that it slices neatly. Serve with berry fruits on the side. Whether you like pavlova or a sweet soufflé, this recipe combines the best of both. You can't get enough of a good thing.

4 egg whites, at room temperature
a pinch of salt
2 cups caster sugar
1 teaspoon cornflour
1½ teaspoons vinegar
½ teaspoon vanilla essence
1¼ cups cream
1 punnet strawberries, hulled and sliced
pulp of 1–2 passionfruit
sifted icing sugar for dusting

SERVES 8

Preheat the oven to 180°C (350°F). Line a 26 x 30 cm Swiss-roll tin with baking paper. Beat the egg whites with salt until stiff peaks form. Beat in 1½ cups of the sugar, 2 tablespoons at a time. Gently fold in the remaining sugar, cornflour, vinegar and vanilla and spoon into the prepared pan. Smooth over surface.

Place in the oven and bake for 12–15 minutes or until set on the top and springy to the touch. Turn out onto a clean tea towel sprinkled generously with caster sugar and leave 5 minutes on a wire rack to cool. Roll up gently from a long end, using the tea towel to assist with the rolling. Leave for 30 minutes or until cool.

Whip the cream to soft peaks, adding half the sliced strawberries and folding them through the cream. Unroll the pavlova, spread with the cream and scatter with more fruit. Roll up again using the tea towel to assist and place seam-side down on a serving plate. Chill for at least 30 minutes and dust with sifted icing sugar to serve. Serve cut into thick slices.

Gateau de Pithiviers

Many years ago, my sister and I had a wonderful holiday touring the Loire Valley — a beautiful part of France. On our way to the little town of Pithiviers we passed through a medieval town where they were celebrating the traditions of bygone times, wearing costumes, beating drums and waving flags. On we went, until we arrived in Pithiviers. It was Sunday lunchtime and the main square was empty. We stood in front of the closed patisserie, which seemed full of the most wonderful-looking pastries, and nearly cried! Then, suddenly, crowds started pouring into the square, coming out of the nearby churches. The charcuterie, boulangerie and patisserie quickly opened and filled with people picking up their special orders. We recovered enough from the commotion to order coffee and Pithiviers and we were not disappointed. The Pithiviers was perfect and, yes, I got the recipe.

Its scalloped edges, domed centre — marked with curved slashes to resemble the petals of a flower — and filling of warm almond paste make Pithiviers one of the world's best pastries.

2 sheets frozen puff pastry made with butter, just thawed
1 egg, beaten with ¼ teaspoon salt, to glaze
caster or sifted icing sugar for dusting

ALMOND FILLING
125 g unsalted butter
½ cup sugar
1 egg
1 egg yolk
125 g whole blanched almonds, freshly ground
1 tablespoon flour
2 tablespoons rum

SERVES 8–10

To prepare the filling, cream the butter in a bowl. Add the sugar and beat until soft and light. Beat in the egg and egg yolk. Stir in the almonds, flour and rum; don't beat the mixture at this point or the oil will be drawn out of the almonds.

Using a cake tin as a guide, use a sharp knife to cut out a 25 cm round from each pastry sheet. Place one round on a baking sheet and mound the filling in the centre, leaving a 2.5 cm border. Brush the border with egg glaze. Lay the other round on top and press the edges together firmly. Scallop the edge of the gâteau by pulling it in at regular intervals with the back of a knife. Brush the gâteau with the egg glaze and, working from the centre, score the top in curves like the petals of a flower without cutting through to the filling. Chill for 15–20 minutes. Preheat the oven to 220°C (430°F).

Pierce a few holes in the centre of the gâteau to allow steam to escape. Sprinkle it with sugar or icing sugar and bake for 20–25 minutes, or until puffed and brown on top. Lower the oven temperature to 200°C (400°F) and continue baking for 15–20 minutes or until firm, lightly browned on the sides and glazed with melted sugar on top. If the sugar has not melted by the time the pastry is cooked, grill it quickly (watching it carefully) until shiny. Cool the gâteau on a rack. Serve warm or at room temperature.

TIP ~ To freshly grind the almonds I use a small nut mill that I have had for years. The next best thing is a coffee grinder, kept especially for grinding nuts, or a food processor. Roughly chop the nuts first by hand, then grind using the pulse button, though not too finely. Little bits of almond give the filling a pleasing texture.

NOTE ~ In France, a version of this cake is made flatter and known as galette des rois (cake of kings). This is a traditional Epiphany cake served on Twelfth Night (6th January), but it's usually available in patisseries from Christmas until the end of January. Traditionally a dried bean or silver trinket would be hidden in the almond paste, and the cake accompanied by a cardboard crown. The lucky person who found the bean in his mouth would wear the crown for the day.

Fruit Soufflé Tart

When making tarts, the French always use whatever fruit is in season, when it is at its peak and cheapest, and are proud of their respect for time, quality ingredients and money. The following tart is regularly made by a member of my family. My own daughter, in spite of having a Scottish mother, also appreciates the value of a beautiful French tart!

Use whatever variety of stone fruit is in season: nectarines, peaches, plums, cherries or apricots.

1 quantity Sweet Flan Pastry (page 202)

FILLING
2 eggs, separated
1/3 cup caster sugar
2 tablespoons plain flour
3/4 cup milk
1 teaspoon vanilla essence
6 ripe nectarines, halved and stoned (or use other fruit in season)
sifted icing sugar for dusting (optional)

SERVES 6-8

Make the pastry, chill for 1 hour or more, and use to line a 23 cm flan tin. Prick the base lightly and chill for about 15 minutes. Meanwhile, preheat the oven to 190°C (375°F). Bake blind (see overleaf for instructions) for about 15 minutes, until the pastry is set. Remove the paper and pastry weights. Return the pastry case to the oven for a further 5 minutes to dry out the base. Cool slightly before filling and baking further.

Increase the oven temperature to 200°C (400°F). To make the filling, beat the egg yolks with the sugar until the mixture forms a ribbon falling into the bowl when the beater is lifted. Stir in the flour. Bring the milk to the boil and pour over the egg-yolk mixture, stirring well until mixed. Add vanilla and transfer the egg-yolk mixture to the saucepan. Cook gently, stirring constantly until thickened, without letting it boil. Remove from the heat and cool to lukewarm, stirring occasionally.

Whisk the egg whites until stiff but not dry and fold them gently into the egg custard. Pour into the prepared flan tin. Arrange the nectarines or other fruit on the egg filling, rounded-side down. Bake for 20 minutes. Reduce oven temperature to 180°C (350°F) and bake for a further 20 minutes or until golden brown. Remove the tart from the oven and dust, if you like, with sifted icing sugar. Serve warm or at room temperature.

Sweet Flan Pastry

1 cup plain flour
pinch of salt
60 g unsalted butter, cut into small pieces
⅓ cup caster sugar
1 teaspoon iced water
2 egg yolks
2 drops vanilla essence

Sift the flour with the salt onto a pastry board or marble slab and make a well in the centre. Place the remaining ingredients in the centre and rub together with the fingertips of one hand. The movement of your fingertips working on these centre ingredients is rather like that of a chicken pecking corn.

Using a metal spatula, quickly draw in the flour. Knead the pastry lightly until smooth. Wrap in plastic wrap and chill for 1 hour or more before using.

Food processor alternative

Chill or freeze the butter. Fit the metal blade attachment. Sift the flour and salt into the food processor bowl. Add the butter and process for 15–20 seconds until the mixture resembles fine breadcrumbs. Add the remaining ingredients and process for a further 20–30 seconds until the mixture starts to cling together. Turn out onto a floured surface and shape into a ball. Knead lightly until smooth, then wrap in plastic wrap and chill before using.

TO BAKE BLIND

When a recipe calls for filling a tart case after it is baked, the pastry usually needs to be baked 'blind'. I like to use soft tissue or greaseproof paper to line the inside of the pastry in the tin. I then fill it to about a quarter with pastry weights or dried beans, so that the pastry keeps its shape while baking. When the pastry is cooked and set, the paper and beans can be removed (and kept for another time) and the pastry returned to the oven to brown a little more.

Fresh Fig and Mascarpone Tart

This fig and mascarpone dessert is hard to beat. I also like to make it with muscat grapes or blueberries, in exactly the same way as set out in this recipe. The pastry is unusual, but it works well with soft fruit tarts such as this one. Small battery-run blowtorches, or gas torches, are available at good kitchen shops or some hardware stores. They are used to caramelise the sugar topping on foods, making a delicious crisp brown crust without heating the food underneath. This can also be done under a hot griller, but care has to be taken not to let the food underneath cook or warm.

2 cups plain flour
½ cup caster sugar
185 g unsalted butter, melted and cooled
a few drops of vanilla essence
1⅓ cups mascarpone, chilled,
    sweetened and flavoured with honey and
    vanilla essence or orange-blossom water
6–8 fresh figs
extra sugar for caramelising (optional)

SERVES 8–10

Preheat the oven to 200°C (400°F). Sift the flour into a bowl and stir in the sugar. Make a well in the centre and add the melted butter and vanilla. Mix together to make a stiff dough. Press the dough into a 25 cm flan tin with removable base, working up the edges evenly. Prick the base well and bake for 15–20 minutes or until golden. Remove from the oven and leave to cool completely.

Whip the chilled mascarpone until it holds its shape. Spread the mascarpone in the tart case as evenly as possible. Quarter the fresh figs and arrange them cut-side up in the tin, as tightly as possible. Serve as is or sprinkle with extra sugar and place under a very hot grill for a minute or so. Alternatively, use a gas torch to caramelise the figs. Serve cut into wedges.

Linzertorte

This Austrian cake is special and quite sophisticated but you don't have to be a pastry cook to make it. If you can make an ordinary butter cake you can certainly make this.

It's worthy of the best china. I get out my old art deco Bavarian tea and coffee service left to me by someone who understood the finer things in life. I could be in one of the grand coffee houses of Austria. How about an einspanner (black coffee with whipped cream and icing sugar) to go with it?

185 g unsalted butter
1 cup caster sugar
grated rind of 1 lemon or ½ teaspoon
    vanilla essence
2 eggs
1¼ cups plain flour
½ teaspoon ground cinnamon
pinch of salt
1¼ cups ground almonds or hazelnuts
½ cup Raspberry Jam (homemade, below,
    or commercial)
sifted icing sugar for dusting

SERVES 12

Preheat the oven to 160°C (320°F). Lightly butter a 23 cm springform tin and line the base with baking paper. Cream the butter with the sugar and beat in the rind or vanilla and the eggs, adding one at a time. Sift the flour with the cinnamon and salt and fold into the creamed mixture with the ground almonds until well mixed.

Spoon one-third of the mixture into a piping bag fitted with a plain 5 mm tube. Spread the remaining mixture into the prepared tin. Gently spread the raspberry jam over the creamed mixture, leaving an edge of 1.5 cm free.

Pipe a ring of mixture around the inside edge of the cake tin, then use the remaining mixture to pipe a lattice over the top, each strip about 2 cm apart. Bake for 30–40 minutes until golden and firm. Leave to cool in the tin a few minutes before removing the base from the tin and cooling the torte on a wire rack. The torte can be served warm or cooled, dusted with icing sugar.

Raspberry Jam

500 g fresh or frozen raspberries
¼ cup lemon juice
1½ cups caster sugar

MAKES ABOUT 1½ CUPS

Combine the raspberries and lemon juice in a large microwave-proof bowl. Microwave on high (100 per cent) power for 5 minutes. Stir in the sugar. Cook on high for another 15–20 minutes, stirring every 5 minutes. Spoon into a sterilised jar, cover and cool before storing.

Financiers

Originally made in a pastry shop near la Bourse, the financial district of Paris, friands — or financiers, as they are often called — are the same shape as gold bars (the moulds are traditionally rectangular).

In Australia, friand moulds are oval in shape and deeper than most other small cake tins. Both are available for purchase at good kitchen shops and department stores. These little almond cakes are very easy to make. No beating is required — the ingredients are simply mixed, then baked.

175 g butter
1 cup ground almonds
grated rind of 1 orange
1²⁄₃ cup sifted icing sugar
⅓ cup + 1 tablespoon plain flour
5 egg whites
200 g fresh or frozen raspberries (optional)
10–12 oval friand moulds or 24 patty-
   pan cases

MAKES 10–12

Preheat the oven to 230°C (445°F). Grease 10–12 friand moulds with butter.

Put the butter in a small saucepan, cook gently until pale gold, and set aside.

Place the ground almonds in a bowl with the orange rind, icing sugar and flour, and mix until combined. Add the egg whites and the warm butter, pouring the butter in carefully and holding back any browned solids that have sunk to the bottom. Mix well together.

Spoon the mixture into the prepared moulds or patty-pan cases, half-filling each. Top each with 2 or 3 raspberries if using, then place the moulds on a baking tray and bake for 5 minutes. Reduce the oven temperature to 200°C (400°F) and bake for a further 12–15 minutes if using moulds. Patty pan cases will take only 8–10 minutes. Turn the oven off and leave the cakes in the oven for 5 minutes. Remove from the oven and turn out onto a cooling rack.

NOTE - A combination of ground pistachios and ground hazelnuts may replace ground almonds for a different look and taste.

Madeleines

These plump little sponge cakes were immortalised in Marcel Proust's novel *Remembrance of Things Past*. They are baked in special embossed moulds that resemble the 'pleated scallop of the pilgrim's shell', which gives them their characteristic puffed dome. Madeleine tins are available in small and large sizes from kitchen shops and department stores.

2 eggs
¾ cup caster sugar
½ teaspoon finely grated lemon rind
1 cup plain flour, sifted
185 g unsalted butter, clarified (see Tip)
1 tablespoon rum (optional)
sifted icing sugar for dusting

MAKES 32 LARGE OR 50 SMALL MADELEINES

Preheat the oven to 200°C (400°F). Butter the madeleine tins and dust them with flour. Beat the eggs and sugar until thick and mousse-like using a hand whisk and a bowl set over a pan of gently simmering water, or a very good electric mixer. Remove from the heat (if using that method) and continue to beat until cooled. Add the lemon rind and fold in the flour and then the cooled butter, mixing only until everything is blended. Take care not to over-work the mixture at this point and don't allow the butter to sink to the bottom of the bowl. A metal spoon or spatula is best for this job. Lastly fold in the rum, if using.

Spoon the mixture into the prepared madeleine tins. Bake large madeleines for 9 minutes or small madeleines for 6–7 minutes until pale golden. Let stand for 1–2 minutes before removing from the tins. Repeat until all the mixture is used. Dust with icing sugar while still warm.

Chocolate madeleines

Sift the flour with 3 tablespoons of cocoa powder to make delicious little chocolate madeleines.

Orange madeleines

Replace lemon rind with grated rind of 1 orange.

TIP ~ To clarify the butter, place in a pan and melt slowly. When the butter is clear remove from the heat, stand for a few minutes and pour the clear butter into a cup, leaving the sediments in the pan. Cool. This can also be done in the microwave.

Sour Cream Chocolate Cake

If I had to choose only one chocolate cake recipe to carry me through life, this would have to be it. It is just as a chocolate cake should be — not the fudgy, flourless kind that everyone loves for dessert, but the perfect cake to slice into wedges for afternoon teas and picnics. The sour cream is the secret to its lightness. The cake cuts easily, yet is rich and beautifully moist. You can keep it plain or add a coating of buttery almonds.

The recipe makes one very large cake or two smaller cakes: one to eat, one to freeze for another time or give to a friend.

4 tablespoons flaked almonds
1 cup boiling water
125 g dark chocolate, chopped
1 teaspoon bicarbonate of soda
250 g unsalted butter
1½ cups caster sugar
3 large eggs, separated
1 teaspoon vanilla essence
2½ cups plain flour
a pinch of salt
1 teaspoon baking powder
⅔ cup light sour cream

SERVES 16–20

Preheat the oven to 180°C (350°F). Generously butter a 3-litre fluted bundt tin or 2 x 20 cm ring tins. Sprinkle with the flaked almonds, pressing them well into the butter to coat the base and sides of the tin.

Put the boiling water, chocolate and bicarbonate of soda in a bowl and stir until the chocolate is melted and smooth. Leave to cool. Cream the butter and sugar until light and fluffy, then add the egg yolks one at a time, beating after each addition. Stir in the vanilla, adding to the chocolate mixture a little at a time. Sift the flour, salt and baking powder and fold in alternately with the sour cream, mixing lightly until just combined. Beat the egg whites until stiff and fold into the mixture with a large metal spoon.

Turn gently into prepared tin(s) and bake for 1–1¼ hours for a large cake, 45 minutes for smaller cakes, or until cooked when tested with a fine skewer. Leave for a minute, then turn out and cool on a wire rack.

Bistro Cheesecake

I've taken in lots of Broadway shows in New York over the years, and often called into the world-famous Lindy's afterwards for a piece of their sinfully rich but heavenly cheesecake. This is as good as it gets, and is a variation of the cheesecake that was so popular in my early days, when I would demonstrate it at Johnny Walker's bistro in Sydney. Until then the flatter European cheesecakes made with more pastry than cheese and from a variety of cheeses like cottage and unrefined cheese were all you could get.

200 g plain biscuits such as Nice,
  crushed or blended into crumbs
6 tablespoons ground almonds
¼ cup cream
75 g butter, melted

FILLING
750 g cream cheese
½ cup caster sugar
2 eggs
grated rind of 1 lemon
1 teaspoon lemon juice
1 teaspoon vanilla essence

TOPPING
1½ cups sour cream
2 tablespoons sugar
½ teaspoon vanilla essence
½ teaspoon grated nutmeg

SERVES 10-12

Line the base of a 23 cm springform tin with baking paper. Stir together the biscuit crumbs, ground almonds, cream and melted butter. Using your fingers, press the crumb mixture into the tin. The crumbs should line the base and come 5 cm up the sides. Chill the crust well while making the filling.

Preheat the oven to 190°C (375°F). Using an electric mixer, beat the cream cheese and sugar until well incorporated, then beat in the eggs, one at a time, adding the lemon rind, juice and vanilla. Pour the cream cheese mixture into the prepared crust and spread evenly with a spatula. Bake for about 20 minutes. Remove from the oven and leave to cool to room temperature.

Increase the oven temperature to 220°C (430°F). Using an electric mixer, beat the sour cream with the sugar and vanilla until smooth. Spoon over the top of the cheesecake and spread evenly. Bake in the oven for about 5 minutes, just enough to glaze. Remove from the oven, cool, then chill for 6–12 hours before serving. The cheesecake may be made a few days ahead and kept covered and chilled. Dust with grated nutmeg to serve, and cut into wedges.

Linda's Orange Cake

The recipe for this cake was given to me by Linda, a New York friend. The orange cake is so orangey and moist and the dark chocolate icing is sublime. It's another family dessert cake we love for special occasions.

Folding in the melted butter requires concentration, and is easiest when the flour is added first. When frosting the cake, turn it out onto a plate with the flat-side uppermost — this seems to be the best side!

1 cup sugar
4 eggs, separated
1 cup plain flour
2 teaspoons baking powder
125 g butter, melted
grated rind and juice of 1 orange
¾ cup orange juice
2 tablespoons sugar

CHOCOLATE ICING
125 g dark chocolate (Club or couverture),
    chopped
1 tablespoon boiling water
1 teaspoon instant coffee
1 tablespoon sour cream

SERVES 8–10

Preheat the oven to 180°C (350°F). Lightly grease a round 20 cm cake tin.

Beat the sugar and egg yolks until thick and creamy. Sift the flour and baking powder and fold into the beaten egg yolks. Fold in the cooled melted butter, orange rind and juice. Beat the egg whites until stiff but not dry and fold into the cake mixture.

Turn the mixture into the prepared cake tin and bake for 40 minutes. Remove from the oven and turn out onto a cake cooler while you combine the orange juice and sugar, stirring briskly until sugar is dissolved.

Return the cake to the tin and while still warm, spoon over the sweetened orange juice. Leave until cold, as the cake will absorb the juice.

To make the icing, place the chocolate in a bowl and stand this over another bowl of hot water. Dissolve the coffee in a tablespoon of boiling water, add to the chocolate and stir until smooth. Remove from the heat and stir in the sour cream until smooth.

Turn the cake out onto a flat plate and spread the top and sides with the prepared chocolate icing. Serve as a dessert with a bowl of unsweetened whipped cream or fresh berries.

Coffee Syrup Cake

Suzanne brought back this recipe from the Cordon Bleu Restaurant in Marylebone Lane, London. Also known as Austrian coffee cake, it's especially moist and has a great flavour, having been soaked in a coffee and rum syrup. It's equally at home at afternoon tea as it is for dessert.

185 g butter
1 cup caster sugar
3 eggs, lightly beaten
1½ cups self-raising flour, sifted
pinch of salt
1–2 tablespoons milk
1¼ cups cream, whipped
½ cup toasted flaked almonds (see Tip)

COFFEE SYRUP
1 cup strong black coffee
75 g sugar
½ cup water
2 tablespoons rum

SERVES 8–10

Preheat the oven to 180°C (350°F). Grease a 5-cup fluted bundt or ring tin (I use a savarin mould).

Cream the butter until soft, then add the sugar, a little at a time, and continue beating until light and fluffy. Gradually add the eggs, beating thoroughly after each addition. Fold in the sifted flour and salt alternately with enough milk to make a dropping consistency.

Spoon into the prepared tin, smooth the top and bake for 40–45 minutes or until a skewer inserted in the centre comes out clean. Leave to cool in the tin for a few minutes, then release the sides a little with the help of a metal spatula and turn out onto a wire rack.

Make the coffee syrup. Put coffee in a heatproof jug. A good instant coffee can be used but make it strong. Heat the sugar and water in a saucepan until the sugar dissolves, then boil for 2 minutes. Add to the coffee and cool. Stir in the rum.

When the cake has cooled, return it to the tin. Slowly pour the coffee syrup over the cake. Cover with plastic wrap and refrigerate until ready to serve. Turn out onto a serving plate and coat with whipped cream and toasted flaked almonds, or serve with a bowl of whipped cream on the side if liked.

TIP - To toast the almonds, spread them on a baking tray and cook in a preheated 180°C (350°F) oven, shaking the tray several times until almonds turn a pale golden. This can be done in a heavy-based frying pan over a gentle heat but watch the almonds don't burn. Cool before using.

Pears in Red Wine

It is hard to resist buying pears when they first appear in shops again after being out of season. There's something about the shape of a pear; it looks perfectly designed, and it is intriguing to see the difference in the shape of each variety. The william is an early-season pear, yellow tinged with pale green, and is usually very juicy. It is delicious eaten with gorgonzola cheese. The winter cole is smaller, round in shape and greenish turning to russet, and pale yellow when ripe. The beurre bosc is elongated with a russet skin turning to a dark cinnamon when mature. The packham, similar in appearance to the william, is greenish-yellow turning to light yellow when ripe. The packham is good for poaching or in a tart.

For poaching, choose pears that are under-ripe but not too hard. Hard pears never seem to soften no matter how long they have been cooked and they just don't have the flavour of fruit that is just about to ripen.

6 small, firm pears of even size
½ cup sugar
1 cup light dry red wine such as pinot noir
strip of lemon rind
small stick cinnamon
1 teaspoon arrowroot (optional)

SERVES 6

Preheat the oven to 180°C (350°F). Peel the pears, but do not remove the stalks. Dissolve the sugar in the wine in a saucepan over a low heat. Add the lemon rind and cinnamon stick. Bring to the boil for 1 minute. Place the pears, stalks up, in a casserole dish and pour over the wine syrup. The pears should just fit so that they all stand up nicely, giving them a better shape when cooked.

Cover the dish and bake for about 1 hour until tender. Remove and strain off the syrup. If necessary, reduce the syrup to make 1 cup. The syrup may be thickened with the arrowroot mixed with a little water. Add the arrowroot to the syrup and stir until almost boiling and quite clear.

Arrange pears in a serving dish and spoon over the wine sauce. They should be served cold and may be accompanied by a bowl of whipped cream, thick cream or mascarpone.

Poached pears

Almost-ripe pears may be cooked on the stove-top in the prepared syrup over a low heat. Remove with a slotted spoon when tender, then reduce the syrup over a high heat and spoon over the pears.

Lemon Delicious Pudding

Generations of readers have written in praising this lemon delicious recipe, sometimes called lemon surprise pudding because underneath the sponge topping is a creamy lemon sauce.

However, the surprise will only be there if the pudding is cooked the right amount. Too much and the sauce will be lost, too little and there won't be enough sponge topping. If there doesn't seem to be enough sponge, return to the oven for a little longer.

60 g butter
grated rind and juice of 1 lemon
⅔ cup sugar
2 eggs, separated
4 tablespoons self-raising flour, sifted
1¼ cups milk

SERVES 6

Preheat the oven to 180°C (350°F). Using an electric mixer, cream the butter with the lemon rind and sugar. When it is creamy and light, beat in the egg yolks. Stir in the sifted flour alternately with the milk.

Beat the egg whites until stiff and fold into the mixture with the lemon juice, lightly yet thoroughly. Pour into a buttered casserole or pie dish and bake for about 45 minutes.

Individual lemon delicious puddings

If you want something that looks a little fancier but tastes just as good, give these a try.

Divide the mixture into 6 individual buttered ramekins and bake in a preheated 180°C (350°F) oven for 20 minutes. Have ready metal skewers that have been heated to red-hot over a naked flame or the stove element. As soon as the puddings come out of the oven, dust the tops with sifted icing sugar. Holding the skewers with an oven mitt, scorch the tops of the puddings quickly with the skewers. Do this one skewer at a time, leaving the other skewers on the heat as you work, to form a crosshatch pattern on the top of each pudding. Serve with thick cream.

Sticky Date Pudding

There's something homely about sticky date pudding. My preferred method of cooking this mixture is in the individual pudding moulds. I use one-cup metal moulds, which I bake for 20–25 minutes. However, you can make one large pudding and bake for 1 hour in a cake tin, then cut into squares. Serve with caramel sauce or thick cream or, better still, with both!

1¼ cups stoned dates
1¼ cups water
1½ teaspoons bicarbonate of soda
125 g unsalted butter, softened
¾ cup caster sugar
3 large eggs
1 teaspoon vanilla essence
2 cups self-raising flour
1 teaspoon ground ginger

CARAMEL SAUCE

1 cup cream
125 g unsalted butter
½ cup soft brown sugar
1 tablespoon golden syrup or maple syrup

SERVES 6–8

Preheat the oven to 180°C (350°F). Grease and line the base of a square 22 cm cake tin. Cover the dates with the water in a small saucepan and bring slowly to the boil. Stir in the bicarbonate of soda and set aside. In the bowl of an electric mixer, beat the butter and sugar until light and fluffy. Add the eggs, one at a time, beating well after each addition, then add the vanilla. Sift the flour with the ginger and fold into the butter mixture. Mash the date mixture with a fork (this can also be done in a food processor). Lightly fold into the batter.

Turn the mixture into the prepared tin and bake for 45 minutes to 1 hour, or until a skewer inserted comes out clean. Let the pudding cool in the tin for 10 minutes, then run a sharp knife around the edge and transfer the pudding, bottom-side down, onto a serving plate.

To make the sauce, combine the cream, butter, brown sugar and golden or maple syrup in a saucepan. Bring the mixture to the boil, stirring, and simmer for 8 minutes over a medium heat, until it thickens slightly. Cut the pudding into squares and pour over caramel sauce to serve.

NOTE ~ This luscious caramel sauce is wonderful served with ice cream or steamed puddings.

Bread and Butter Pudding

I thought I knew how to make a good bread and butter pudding until I went to the American state of Louisiana in the 1980s as a guest of the McIlhenny (Tabasco) family. This old-fashioned British pudding has become the 'belle' of America's south, where it is usually spiked with bourbon. I've been adding a wee dram of whisky (I am a Scot after all) to this ultimate in comfort food ever since.

It's usually made using leftover bread and milk, and is richer with cream. It makes a big difference when the prepared pudding is left to stand for 15 minutes before baking, so the bread can soak up the custard, giving it a sumptuous but light finish.

Even an old-fashioned bread and butter pudding like this has plenty of scope for cooks and chefs to update with their own special touch. Some recipes and restaurants use brioche, croissants or fruit loaf, but I prefer the simplicity of a good white loaf, thickly sliced.

12 slices white bread
60 g soft butter
1 cup sultanas
2 tablespoons currants (optional)
4–6 eggs, lightly beaten
½ cup sugar
½ cup whisky, bourbon or sherry
½ teaspoon grated mace or nutmeg
3½ cups milk
1 cup cream
1 teaspoon ground cinnamon sifted
   icing sugar for dusting (optional)

SERVES 6

Preheat the oven to 190°C (375°F). Butter the bread, first removing the crusts, if you like. Cut into triangles and arrange in a large, buttered ovenproof dish. Scatter with the fruit. Beat the eggs with the sugar and alcohol, and mace or nutmeg. Scald the milk with the cream and pour the hot liquid into the egg mixture, mixing well.

Strain over the bread triangles and leave to soak for 10–15 minutes. Sprinkle with cinnamon. Set the dish in a baking dish of hot water that reaches halfway up the sides of the pudding dish and bake until a knife inserted in the centre comes out clean and the pudding is risen and golden. This can take 45 minutes to an hour. Dust with icing sugar, if liked, and serve.

Chocolate Soufflés

The famous French soufflé is one of the lightest, most delectable and useful dishes in a cook's repertoire. Any chef worth their salt can whip up a soufflé on demand and with today's excellent thermostatically controlled ovens it is easier to succeed than to fail in making soufflés.

For chocolate soufflés I like to use individual dishes and choose quality dark chocolate. For an even more chocolatey flavour I also use a good Dutch cocoa. Don't be afraid. There's nothing more to making a soufflé than there is to lightening custard with whipped egg whites, and baking it.

100 g dark chocolate, chopped
⅓ cup icing sugar
75 g unsalted butter
3 tablespoons plain flour
¼ cup cocoa powder
1 cup milk
a pinch of salt
2 tablespoons rum or brandy,
　or 1 teaspoon vanilla essence
4 egg yolks
5 egg whites
¼ teaspoon cream of tartar
thick cream and icing sugar for
　dusting (optional)

SERVES 6

Preheat the oven to 190°C (375°F). Melt the chocolate in a heatproof bowl set over a saucepan of hot, but not boiling water. Butter 6 x 1-cup soufflé dishes or ramekins and dust the insides with a tablespoon of the measured icing sugar. Place on a baking tray and set aside.

Melt the butter in a saucepan over a low heat and stir in the flour and cocoa powder until blended. Add the milk and continue to stir, increasing heat to medium, until a smooth, thick sauce forms. Add a pinch of salt, the melted chocolate and the rum or other flavouring, stirring until the mixture is smooth. Cool for 5 minutes then whisk in the egg yolks, one at a time. The soufflé mixture can be made in advance to this point.

Whisk the egg whites and cream of tartar until soft peaks form, then gradually beat in the remaining icing sugar until stiff but not dry. Stir a large dollop of the egg-white mixture into the chocolate mixture and then gently fold in the remainder using a large metal spoon.

Turn the mixture into the prepared dishes and smooth the tops. Bake for about 20 minutes until risen and set, then transfer to warm plates and serve immediately. You can, if you like, cut a slit in the tops of the soufflés on serving and add a dollop of thick cream, then sift a little icing sugar over the top.

Self-saucing Chocolate Pudding

I just can't imagine who created this recipe. It seems such an extraordinary thing to do — pouring hot water over a chocolate pudding — but people love it, especially when it is baked in individual dishes.

One ingredient that makes a difference is a good-quality Dutch cocoa. Years ago I bought a pretty tin of Van Houten's Dutch Cocoa and have been extolling its virtues ever since. Look for it in the specialty kitchen supply shops or good delis.

1 cup self-raising flour
2 tablespoons cocoa powder
125 g butter
½ cup caster sugar
2 eggs, lightly beaten
½ teaspoon vanilla essence
½ cup milk

SAUCE
½ cup brown sugar
1 tablespoon cocoa powder
2 cups hot water

SERVES 4–5

Preheat the oven to 200°C (400°F). Lightly butter a 4–5 cup soufflé dish or 4 or 5 x 250 ml soufflé dishes or ovenproof bowls.

Sift the flour and cocoa together and set aside. In the bowl of an electric mixer cream the butter and sugar until light and fluffy, then add the eggs and vanilla, mixing well. Lightly fold in the flour and cocoa mixture alternately with the milk. Spoon into the prepared soufflé dishes.

To make the sauce, combine the sugar and cocoa in a small bowl and sprinkle over the pudding mixture. Carefully pour the hot water over the puddings. Bake for 30–35 minutes for a large pudding and 20–25 minutes for individual puddings. Serve warm with whipped cream.

Rhubarb and Strawberry Crumble

Sweetened adequately, rhubarb is absolutely luscious, and is at last getting the attention it deserves. Surprisingly, rhubarb is also a great mixer. Not only do I love to combine it with apple but it is also wonderful with oranges or strawberries. If you find rhubarb on its own too tart, it can be mellowed by adding an equal amount of apple.

½ cup sugar
juice and rind of 1 orange
1 bunch rhubarb, trimmed and cut into
    5 cm lengths
1 punnet strawberries, washed, hulled
    and halved

CRUMBLE TOPPING
1 cup plain flour
60 g butter
¼ cup sugar
½ teaspoon ground cinnamon
⅓ cup desiccated coconut

SERVES 4-6

Preheat the oven to 180°C (350°F). Combine the sugar and orange juice in a saucepan. Stir over a medium heat until the sugar dissolves. Bring to the boil, then lower the heat and add the rhubarb and orange rind. Cover and simmer for 5 minutes, or until tender but not mushy. Stir in the strawberries.

Make the crumble topping. Sift the flour into a bowl, and rub the butter into it until the mixture resembles coarse breadcrumbs. Add the sugar, cinnamon and coconut and mix well.

Spoon the fruit into a greased ovenproof dish. Sprinkle with the crumble topping and bake until golden brown, for about 30 minutes. If liked, serve with thick cream, natural yoghurt or vanilla ice cream.

Basics

Mayonnaise

When I discovered the recipe for proper French mayonnaise there was no going back and I included it in my first cookbook in the late 1960s. With its sumptuous texture and fresh, subtle flavour, it takes only about 10 minutes to make by hand once you've mastered the technique and is faster still with a food processor.

2 egg yolks
½ teaspoon salt
a pinch of freshly ground black pepper
1 teaspoon Dijon mustard or ½ teaspoon
   dry mustard
2 teaspoons white wine vinegar or
   lemon juice
¾ cup light olive oil or rice bran oil
¼ cup extra-virgin olive oil

MAKES ABOUT 1 CUP

Ensure all ingredients are at room temperature. Warm the eggs and oil in hot water if they are cold. Rinse a mixing bowl with hot water, dry it and wrap a damp cloth around the base to keep it steady.

Place the egg yolks, salt, pepper, mustard and 1 teaspoon of the vinegar or lemon juice in the bowl and beat with a wire whisk or hand-held blender to combine. When the mixture is thick, begin to add the oil, drop by drop, whisking constantly and incorporating thoroughly before adding the next drop. As the mixture thickens, the oil flow can be increased to a steady thin stream, but you must keep beating constantly. When all the oil is incorporated, including the extra-virgin olive oil, beat in the remaining vinegar or lemon juice. Store in a cool place, covered.

TIP ~ If the mayonnaise refuses to thicken, or if it curdles, take a clean, warmed bowl and beat an egg yolk with ½ teaspoon each of salt and vinegar, then gradually beat in the curdled mayonnaise, very slowly at first, then more quickly.

Mayonnaise made in a food processor or blender

Place a whole egg, seasonings and 1 teaspoon of the vinegar or lemon juice in the bowl of a food processor and blend for a few seconds. With the motor running, add 1 cup of oil gradually, ensuring that each addition has been blended before adding more. When all the oil has been incorporated, add the remaining vinegar or lemon juice.

Lime mayonnaise

Add the juice of 1 lime and a little of the grated rind in place of the vinegar or lemon juice. Try adding chopped coriander when serving with seafood.

Sesame mayonnaise

Instead of the extra-virgin olive oil, use rice bran oil or a light olive oil and add a few drops of sesame oil and a tablespoon of lightly ground toasted sesame seeds. This mayonnaise is great with chicken or seafood salads.

Garlic mayonnaise (aïoli)

This is one of the best-loved sauces of France. Crush 3 or 4 cloves of garlic to a paste with a little salt (this can be done with the flat of a knife blade on a chopping board). Transfer to a bowl. Add the 2 egg yolks and seasonings as for the basic recipe. Alternatively, if making in a food processor add the garlic with the egg and proceed with the recipe. Serve with poached chicken, fish or raw vegetables.

Pesto alla Genovese

Pesto sauce was created by the Genovese of Italy's north to serve with all kinds of pasta and gnocchi, but is now eaten all over the western world. It is added to soups, especially thick vegetable ones, smeared on bruschetta or toasts for quick appetisers or canapés, and even drizzled over meats.

Traditionally, pesto is made with basil leaves, but a greener and lighter version can be made by replacing some or all of the basil leaves with parsley or mint. Today it is even made with rocket or coriander and the traditional pine nuts are often replaced with walnuts or pistachios.

It's worthwhile having a jar of it in the fridge to transform everyday foods into something special. Remember to keep it covered with a film of oil.

2 cloves garlic, chopped
4 cups basil leaves
2 cups flat-leaf parsley
2 tablespoons pine nuts
½ cup grated parmesan cheese
sea salt and freshly ground black pepper
1 cup olive oil

MAKES 1½ CUPS

Place the garlic, herbs, pine nuts, parmesan, salt and pepper in a food processor and process, scraping down the sides of the bowl once or twice, until finely chopped. With the motor still running, add the oil in a slow, steady stream and process to a smooth paste, similar in consistency to mayonnaise.

Spoon into jars, covering with a thin film of oil before topping with a lid. Keep in the refrigerator.

Mint pesto
Make as for pesto alla Genovese, substituting 2 cups of mint leaves for the basil and add an extra cup of flat-leaf parsley.

Rocket and walnut pesto
Make as for pesto alla Genovese, substituting rocket leaves for the basil and chopped walnuts for the pine nuts.

Pistachio pesto
Make as for pesto alla Genovese, replacing the pine nuts with pistachio nuts, which have been blanched in hot water for 2 minutes, drained, then rubbed briskly to remove skins.

STOCK, BROTH OR BOUILLON

Stock, broth or bouillon is the clear, flavourful liquid that you get after various meats and vegetables have been simmered in water and then strained. Stock made from beef is brown or light golden; chicken makes a white stock; fish a clear stock. Each has its uses.

When making stock, choose a saucepan with a flat base and a close-fitting lid. You don't want the precious liquid to evaporate too quickly and fill the kitchen with steam. In many recipes a particular stock is needed, but where unspecified, use chicken, beef or vegetable — keep fish for seafood dishes. Stocks last for a week in the refrigerator, and they can also be frozen for up to two months.

Beef Stock

1.5 kg beef bones (shank, marrow bone
    or rib bones or a combination)
500 g cubed shin of beef
1 carrot, thickly sliced
1 onion, thickly sliced
2 teaspoons salt
1 teaspoon black peppercorns
bouquet garni (see page 15)

Ask your butcher to crack the bones. Remove any large pieces of meat and chop finely. Place bones, beef and vegetables in a large baking dish and brown in a preheated oven at 190°C (375°F) for about 20 minutes. This gives the stock a rich brown colour and improves the flavour. Transfer to a large saucepan, add salt, peppercorns and bouquet garni. Cover with cold water. Bring slowly to the boil, skim surface well, and simmer very gently, half-covered, for 3–4 hours (very slow simmering for a long time is the secret). Strain through a fine sieve, cool, then chill in the refrigerator. Remove the surface fat before using.

Chicken Stock

500 g chicken bones (thighs, with bones, necks,
    wings or backs or a chicken carcass)
1 teaspoon salt
1 small carrot, thickly sliced
1 small onion, thickly sliced
bouquet garni (see page 15)

Place bones in a large heavy-based saucepan and add remaining ingredients. Cover with cold water and bring to the boil, carefully skimming the surface. Cover pan and simmer gently for 1–2 hours. Strain through a fine sieve and cool. Refrigerate until needed. Before using, skim off any solidified fat from the surface.

CLARIFYING STOCK

This is needed when making consommé or aspic. Discard all fat and place the cold stock in a saucepan with 2 lightly beaten egg whites, and the 2 egg shells, crushed a little. Bring slowly to the boil, whisking occasionally with a balloon whisk. Let the liquid rise in the pan as it reaches boiling point, then lower the heat, and simmer very gently for 20 minutes.

You will find that as the egg whites cook they attract and hold any remaining particles of fat and residue that might cloud the stock. Strain through a colander lined with muslin, and you have a clear liquid.

Fish Stock

1–2 kg bones, heads (without gills) or trimmings
   of any white, non-oily fish
1 cup white wine, or the juice of a lemon plus
   water to make 1 cup
1 teaspoon white peppercorns
bouquet garni (see page 15)

Put all the ingredients in a saucepan, cover with cold water and bring to the boil. Skim the surface, and simmer very gently for 20 minutes. Strain through a fine sieve.

TIP ~ Fish stock must be simmered, never boiled. Do not throw away crab, lobster or prawn (shrimp) heads. Put them in the freezer in plastic bags; they will keep there and be ready to toss in the stockpot when you need some fish stock.

Vegetable Stock

1 onion, chopped
1 leek, trimmed, washed, then cut into
   thick slices
3 stalks celery, chopped
1 parsnip or turnip, washed
1 piece ginger (walnut-size), finely chopped
bouquet garni (see page 15)
12 black peppercorns
1 teaspoon salt

Put all the ingredients in a large saucepan or stockpot. Cover with cold water and bring to the boil. Lower heat and simmer, partially covered, for about 1 hour. Pour the stock through a colander set over another container, pressing the vegetables against the sides of the colander to extract the juices; discard the solids. Pour through a strainer, cool and refrigerate.

NOTE ~ If freezing stock, always chill first, then remove the fat that floats to the surface. Freeze stock in 1-cup size containers and date them. These are handy amounts for cooking soups and also vegetables like leeks, fennel and peas, as well as meat or poultry. For freezing small amounts of stock use ice cube trays. As soon as the cubes are frozen they can be tipped into a freezer bag.

Cook's notes

The metric weights and liquid measures used in this book are those of the Standards Association of Australia.

To make these recipes you need a few inexpensive pieces of equipment obtainable at most supermarkets.

These are:
~ A standard graduated 250 ml fluid measuring jug for measuring liquids.
~ A nest of 4 graduated metric measuring cups comprising: 250 ml cup, ½, ⅓ and ¼ cup — used for measuring dry ingredients.
~ A set of standard measuring spoons comprising: 1 tablespoon (20 ml), 1 teaspoon (5 ml), ½ teaspoon (2.5 ml) and ¼ teaspoon (1.25 ml).

NOTE: North American and British measuring cups and spoons vary from Australian standards. Follow one set of measures; do not mix them.

~ A small set of scales.
~ A measuring tape or ruler that gives both metric and imperial measurements.

How to measure correctly

DRY INGREDIENTS: In measuring dry ingredients (flour, sugar, etc.) heap the cup or spoon and level off the excess with a knife or spatula.

LIQUID INGREDIENTS: The metric measuring cup shows 1 cup, ¾, ⅔, ½, ¼ and ⅛ cup measures and their metric equivalents. The litre jug has a similar breakdown from litre to ¼ litre and also shows graduations in millilitres (1000 ml — 4 cups — 1 litre). All cup and spoon measures are level.

~ The recipes in this book have been made with the 250 ml cup.
~ 55–60 g eggs have been used unless otherwise specified.
~ The term 'spring onions' is used to describe the non-bulbous fresh green onion (also known as a shallot).
~ Can, pack and bottle sizes are given in metric. Some cans and packs may vary a little from exact sizes given according to the different brands available. It is best to use the nearest size.

Abbreviations used

gram	g
kilogram	kg
centimetre	cm
millimetre	mm
millilitre	ml

Oven temperature guide

Oven temperatures are expressed in degrees Celsius (°C) and in degrees Fahrenheit (°F). If using a fan-forced oven, as a guide, drop the temperature by 20°C. Oven temperatures vary according to make; therefore, refer to the instruction book that accompanies each oven. All ovens should be preheated to the specified temperature particularly for cakes, biscuits and pastry recipes.

Conversion tables

WEIGHT

Metric	Imperial
10–15 g	½ oz
20 g	¾ oz
30 g	1 oz
40 g	1½ oz
50–60 g	2 oz
75 g	2½ oz
80 g	3 oz
100 g	3½ oz
125 g	4 oz
150 g	5 oz
175 g	6 oz
200 g	7 oz
225 g	8 oz
250 g	9 oz
275 g	10 oz
300 g	10½ oz
350 g	12 oz
400 g	14 oz
450 g	1 lb
500 g	1 lb 2 oz
600 g	1 lb 5 oz
650 g	1 lb 7 oz
750 g	1 lb 10 oz
900 g	2 lb
1 kg	2 lb 3 oz

VOLUME

Metric	Imperial
50–60 ml	2 fl oz
75 ml	2½ fl oz
100 ml	3½ fl oz
120 ml	4 fl oz
150 ml	5 fl oz
170 ml	6 fl oz
200 ml	7 fl oz
225 ml	8 fl oz
250 ml	8½ fl oz
300 ml	10 fl oz
400 ml	13 fl oz
500 ml	17 fl oz
600 ml	20 fl oz
750 ml	25 fl oz
1 litre	34 fl oz

LENGTH

Metric	Imperial
5 mm	¼ in
1 cm	½ in
2 cm	¾ in
2.5 cm	1 in
5 cm	2 in
7.5 cm	3 in
10 cm	4 in
15 cm	6 in
20 cm	8 in
30 cm	12 in

Index

A lifetime of writing

The Margaret Fulton Cookbook, 1968

Margaret Fulton's Ice Cream Wonderland, 1970

The Woman's Day Cookbook, 1970

Canned Fruit and Meat Recipe Book, 1971

Entertaining with Margaret Fulton, 1971

Margaret Fulton Cookery Course, 1973

Margaret Fulton's Favourite Recipes, 1973

Margaret Fulton's Italian Cookbook, 1973

The Complete Margaret Fulton Cookbook, 1974

Margaret Fulton's Crockpot Cookbook, 1976

Cooking for Good Health, 1978

Margaret Fulton Oven Magic, 1978

My Very Special Cookbook, 1980

The Margaret Fulton Creative Cooking Course, 1981

Superb Restaurant Dishes, 1982

Cooking for Family and Friends, 1983

The Everyday Cookery Book, 1983

Margaret Fulton's Encyclopedia of Food and Cookery, 1983

The New Idea Cookbook, 1986

Margaret Fulton's Book of Cooking for Two, 1989

Margaret Fulton's New Cookbook, 1993

Cooking for One and Two, 1995

A Passionate Cook, 1998

I Sang for My Supper: Memoirs of a Food Writer, 1999

Cooking for Dummies (co-author Barbara Beckett), 2001

Margaret Fulton's Kitchen, 2007

Margaret Fulton Christmas, 2008

Note: The year indicates the first year of publication.
Many of these books have since been fully revised and updated.

Acknowledgments

Suzanne and I would like to express our thanks to the Hardie Grant Books team for suggesting there should be a book about my recipes that have stood the test of time.

Many people have turned our words into a book to be loved and cherished: publisher Mary Small, who conceived and developed the idea; Tanya Zouev, a talented photographer who photographed the food; and Caroline Velik, who cooked and styled the food at the photography shoot.

We owe a huge debt of gratitude to the many generous people who loaned us equipment and props to enhance the photography: Bliink Interiors, Designer Laminates, Great Dane Furniture, Höganäs ceramics from Jarass, and Riess enamelware from Crowley and Grouch.

A special word of thanks goes to our dear friend Jannie Brown, who opened her lovely home to us for the photography shoot. It really does make a difference to work in a pleasant, happy atmosphere.

This book is about food, life and sharing and
is dedicated to our dear friend Jannie Brown.

First published in 2007 as *Margaret Fulton's Kitchen*

This edition published in 2010 by
Hardie Grant Books
85 High Street
Prahran, Victoria 3181, Australia
www.hardiegrant.com.au

Cover and internal design concept: Steve Smedley
Designer: Susanne Geppert
Photography: Tanya Zouev, Armelle Habib (p9, 10-11, 50-51, 76,
80-81, 132, 134-135, 137, 143, 155, 178-179, 223, 230-231, 235,
238, 240-241, 242, 245, 252, 255)
Stylist: Caroline Velik

Cataloguing-in-Publication data is available from the National
Library of Australia.

ISBN 13: 978 174066 906 1

Colour reproduction by Splitting Image Colour Studio
Printed and bound in China by C&C Offset Printing.

Copyright text © Margaret Fulton 2007
Copyright photographs © Tanya Zouev 2007

Page 4: From the library of Margaret Fulton: the first page of a
handwritten cookbook created for the Duke of Norfolk's estate,
dated 1733.